FREEDOM FROM FEAR

Also by Mark McDonald

United States of Fear: How America Fell Victim to a Mass Delusional Psychosis

FREEDOM FROM FEAR

A 12 STEP GUIDE TO PERSONAL AND NATIONAL RECOVERY

MARK McDONALD M.D.

Published by Bombardier Books
An Imprint of Post Hill Press
ISBN: 978-1-63758-620-4
ISBN (eBook): 978-1-63758-621-1

Freedom from Fear:
A 12 Step Guide to Personal and National Recovery

Cover Design by Matt Margolis
Interior Design by Yoni Limor

Post Hill Press
New York • Nashville
posthillpress.com

Published in the United States of America
1 2 3 4 5 6 7 8 9 10

Contents

Introduction

The Fear Addiction 7

Step 1

Face the Mirror: Admit You Are an Addict 17

Step 2

Don't Be a Sheep: Reject the Collective 25

Step 3

Live in the Real World: Choose Reality Over Fantasy 35

Step 4

Reject Narcissism: Your Fear Doesn't Matter to Society ... 47

Step 5

Cut Off the Dealer: Eliminate Media Fear Junkies 61

Step 6

Think for Yourself: Or Others Will Think for You 73

Step 7

Accountability: Acknowledge the Harm Your Fear Has Caused Yourself and Others 83

Step 8

Embrace Adulthood: Find a Proper Way to Care for Those You Love 93

Step 9

Overrule Your Emotions: Act in Spite of Your Fear 103

Step 10

Find Perspective: Develop a Sense of Humor 113

Step 11

Pay Attention: Give the Gift of Your Full Presence 121

Step 12

Display Fearless Leadership: Grow Your Courage by Mentoring Others. 131

Conclusion

Towards a National Recovery 139

About the Author **143**

Introduction

The Fear Addiction

I went to dinner at a restaurant recently and walked past a mother and daughter waiting for the restroom. Both were wearing masks. I turned to the daughter, no more than ten or twelve years old, and asked, "Why are you wearing that on your face?" Unable to answer, she looked up at her mother for help. What came out of her mother's mouth was an incoherent, hysterical tirade—a jumbled mess of nonsensical phrases like "observing safety," "closing schools," and "ensuring compliance." Nothing she said sounded rational or well-considered in any way. She ended with this: "You have no right to interfere in our lives and intrude into the decisions of our family." She then dragged her daughter into the restroom, clutching her to her chest for dear life, and locked the door behind both of them.

The story doesn't end there, though. After I returned to my table on the outdoor patio, a tense, frantic man appeared. He was looking for something, or someone. He approached me and demanded to know if I was the person who had just spoken to his wife. After I acknowledged that I was, he proceeded to explain that he was a nonmedical professor in a clinical department at the University of California, Los Angeles, and that "all of my colleagues tell me that masking children is perfectly safe." I let him speak for several minutes before interrupting him to ask, "And how do *you* feel about ordering your daughter to wear a mask?" His response? "I feel nothing." He then demanded that I apologize to his wife for the emotional upset I had caused her. When I refused, he stormed out, muttering something about "needing to take action…manager… police…consequences."

After the husband ran off, the couple sitting at the table next to mine turned around, and the woman said, "How awful and rude. This man is sick. We would never do something like that to our child. We're from Orange County, and even though we had some legitimate concerns at the beginning of all this, we knew our children would be fine, and we're certainly not afraid of anything now."

The experience I had at the restaurant illustrates the growing divide in the United States between those who have emerged from under the blanket of fear and those who seem unable to let go of it. For this latter group, fear appears to be (oddly) a source of security. What is wrong with these people?

More than two years have passed since the pandemic began, and it ended more than one year ago, yet a large swath of the U.S. population has chosen to continue to live in fear. Their decision defies all reason, logic, science, and common sense.

Some may be completely unaware of the choice they have made to live in fear. They have become so conditioned to live, breathe, speak, and act in fear that they have lost access to a healthy baseline of what a non-fear-based life looks like. They are like an alcoholic who carries a flask in his breast pocket, nurses it throughout the day, and believes this to be normal behavior.

Over the past several years, many Americans have become addicted to fear. This is clear from the ubiquitous sightings of lone drivers wearing masks in their cars, or individuals stepping into the street to avoid passing by another person on the sidewalk. Many adults now refuse to return to the office, voluntarily continuing to work from home, not for convenience but due to an unshakable discomfort about spending time in a room with other people every day. I see it expressed in children as well, many of whom feel terrified at the prospect of attending a sleepover, having spent nearly two years confined to their homes, unable to attend school or play with friends. More than half of Los Angeles residents polled before the Super Bowl in 2022 reported that they would be watching the event alone or only with immediate family due to their discomfort about celebrating the game with a large group. Americans have become so used to fear-driven behaviors that they have developed a dependency on them, and the thought of ending them produces a withdrawal response.

Even now, as ludicrous and destructive mandates are suddenly lifted throughout the country (for purely political reasons), few Americans are choosing to return to a truly normal way of life. Many of those living in cities have shown themselves to be incapable of making informed decisions—they continue to wear masks wherever they go, eschew a healthy diet and regular exercise, and refuse to travel outside the confines of their neighborhood. The primary driver of weight gain today is empty calories: alcohol and nutrient-deficient foods that provide temporary comfort at the expense of long-term health. A young woman whose employer announced an end to mandatory mask-wearing at work recently told me she would continue to wear one anyway, "because I have babies at home." Her coworker said, "I'm not wearing one to work, but I'll put it on when I go to crowded places." Both women are in their twenties and appear to be quite healthy, yet have adopted the ridiculous practice of covering their faces with a piece of dirty cloth because they believe the world they live in is no longer safe. They live in fear today because they cannot think critically.

For some, particularly those living in a small town or rural America, fear addiction is a nonissue. They don't rely on mainstream media to be informed, and they don't look to the government to keep themselves safe. Their focus is on work, family, and church. They know how to accurately assess risk because they maintain a close relationship with their community and the natural environment. They have been inoculated against fear.

For others, fear may be endemic in their family, circle of friends, and larger community. This is the reality in most urban areas in the United States today. While some larger cities, such as Tampa, have weathered the fear pandemic well, most have not. New York, Los Angeles, Chicago, and Washington, D.C., for example, have not fared well. Although government-imposed isolation is receding, large swaths of the population continue to lead lives of self-imposed, fear-driven isolation and disconnection from their communities. Even friends and family remain cut off from many. Although normalized in urban areas, this unhealthy behavior is viewed by healthy Americans as bizarre and unexplainable. What has gone wrong with these people?

The answer is simple: They are addicted to fear.

Fear can become an addiction. Just like gambling, sex, drugs, and video games, fear-based behaviors can spin out of control and damage the addict, as well as those close to him. Simply put, an addiction is an out-of-control, recurring behavior that causes harm: use despite harm and loss of control. None of the practices listed above necessarily lead to addiction, however. Many people enjoy a glass of wine without becoming an alcoholic. Placing a wager on the Super Bowl does not mean you are addicted to gambling. Unfortunately, these activities often do lead to addiction because of the way they affect our brain chemistry. One of the most recent addictions to plague society is the cell phone. It is not the phone itself that creates problems but rather the sophisticated apps like TikTok, Instagram, and Snapchat that capture the user's attention and manipulate the brain in a way that deprives the user of his ability to easily disengage.

All addictions are mediated by a neurotransmitter in the brain called dopamine. Dopamine is known as the pleasure or reward signal and is produced during activities like exercise, sex, or smoking. The pleasurable feeling that comes from dopamine release becomes linked, over time, to the behavior that produced it, regardless of whether that behavior is truly healthy. Pleasure and health are often not related, which is why even harmful, self-destructive behaviors can be reinforced if they happen to be pleasurable at the moment.

Cell phone software, for example, has been designed to provoke repeated small releases of dopamine through push notifications, "likes," beeps, and other "rewards" that come both randomly and as a result of active use of the phone. Complex algorithms tease users with rewards after an extended period of inactivity as an incentive to return to the device, increasing in frequency during active use to extend the period of engagement as long as possible. As the business model of these applications relies on either ad revenue or the procurement of user data (or both) for growth, cultivating cell phone addiction is in the developers' best interests. It enables these products to continue to gain market share, even while they wreck the lives of their consumers, who develop anxiety, depression, insomnia, and autistic social behaviors that handicap their growth and development.

Certainly, cell phones have brought conveniences into our lives; however, the social cost has been high. It would be fair and accurate to describe the role of the cell phone software developer as that of a drug dealer, and the electronic rewards the software provides as the drug. Whether a phone, a bottle of whiskey, or a roulette table, the mechanism of addiction is the same—the user is lured by a pleasurable experience and then chemically captured by it, obliged to return for more.

Soon, habituation and dependency develop. Habituation is what happens when you get used to an experience and begin to feel less excited by it the more you participate in it. Having chocolate cake for dessert every night would not be nearly as enjoyable after a full week of eating it once a day. You might even decide to increase the size of the slice to see if eating more would bring you the same level of enjoyment that you felt on day one. As long as you continue to eat the cake every day, though, no matter how much you eat, it's unlikely you will ever enjoy it as much as you did the first time. Eventually, you may decide simply to give up cake entirely. "Today, it's over," you promise. "No more cake for dessert." So that night you skip the cake, and everything goes well. You feel great at giving up something that had simply grown to be a habit (and was leading you to put on extra weight).

Strangely, though, the following night, you notice that after finishing dinner you are craving the cake again. You feel unfulfilled, as if something is missing. Whether you realize it or not, you have developed a dependency on chocolate cake—when you forgo eating it, you experience the discomfort of withdrawal, the physical and psychological effects of removing an addictive substance from your body (or removing an addictive behavior from your daily routine). Habituation, dependency, and withdrawal are always part of the addiction cycle.

Addiction involves a complex interaction between behavior and brain chemistry. Addiction behaviors always provide immediate comfort at the expense of long-term health. The behaviors require an increasing degree of use to maintain their comforting effects, and stopping them provokes an uncomfortable, even painful experience that often leads to a resumption of the behaviors. This process is no different when it comes to fear addiction. Fear is a drug, one that many Americans have become addicted to. They can choose to overcome their addiction, though, if they are motivated to put in the necessary work. The question is how to proceed.

The most famous and successful program ever developed to combat addiction is Alcoholics Anonymous. AA makes the road to recovery manageable through a prescribed series of steps followed in the proper order. Anyone can try to overcome addiction through pure willpower, but a journey undertaken without a map rarely ends at the desired destination. This book provides that map.

The twelve-step model is effective for several reasons. First, it is peer-based. No clinician is ordering you to do anything. You participate voluntarily and are held accountable for your actions by others who are facing the same challenges as you. It also demands that you acknowledge the existence of a higher power located outside of yourself that you must look to for guidance and strength. This counters the inherent narcissism of addiction: "My feelings and experiences are more important than anything or anyone else." Finally, it is methodical. It begins with the acknowledgment of the addiction, progresses through increasingly more difficult and sophisticated stages, and concludes with the never-ending step of passing along what you have learned to others. The twelve-step model is not scientific, but it is humanistic. Its focus is on the fragility and the potential of each individual human being. Most important, it is grounded in reality, where all truth originates. That is the starting point for all my work as a clinical psychiatrist, as well as for my program to overcome fear addiction.

Taking inspiration from Jordan Peterson's *12 Rules for Life*, my program also provides a psychological rationale for holding yourself accountable to the inescapable constraints of reality. Today, many people struggle with accepting reality because doing so confers responsibility. Yet accountability is a prerequisite for any worthwhile teaching program, and one can never be truly free without embracing it. My recommended approach also incorporates the cognitive-behavioral therapy (CBT) model of treating mental illness, with a focus on behavior. Thinking alone does not enable recovery. Action must drive the process. Only by acting in spite of your fear can lasting change occur.

This book is written for those who have developed an addiction to fear and wish to recover from it. It requires a will to change and a curiosity for a fear-free life. It also requires courage—courage to abandon the quasicomforts of a life lived in relative isolation from society at large. In short, it demands that you accept reality and the responsibilities that come with it.

Few people intend to become an addict. As with any chemical drug, though, the first experience of fear provides a rush. It's exciting. It offers an escape from the dreary quotidian routine of life. The price paid comes only later, as chronic fear debilitates the psyche and the body. More powerful than either love or hate, fear—once invited in—makes itself at home and refuses to leave, despite repeated requests by its host. Fear is the most powerful emotion. This book is for those who have suffered from the destructive effects of fear, have grown weary of them, and now want to move forward with their lives. Perhaps they have hit rock bottom. Recovery is their only option.

Those who have been brainwashed to believe that fear is both necessary and virtuous cannot be helped with a recovery manual. Like members of a cult who swear allegiance to a guru and have cut off every healthy relationship, they are unreachable in their current environment. Until and unless they leave the cult, the only effective method of helping them is deprogramming. They must be physically removed from the offending environment against their will, and forcefully reintroduced to reality. This is no small task, and I will not attempt to describe it here.

As for those who have orchestrated the fear pandemic, these individuals suffer from a sociopathic personality disorder. Overcome by their own narcissism and absence of conscience, they press forward with their campaign to addict every living human being to unmanageable fear. They desire to put a needle of fear in every arm. They are the drug dealers whose only concern is growing their base of users. They have brought evil upon the world and can be stopped only by physical and judicial compulsion. The project of individual and national recovery that is so urgently needed today threatens their power because it offers their customers an exit from the endless cycle of fear they are peddling. These people are not misguided, nor are they victims. They are evil. And amorality cannot be remedied through education.

In *United States of Fear*, I traced the cultural antecedents of the explosion of fear throughout America in early 2020. This fear was not new. It had been growing for decades. And just as the fear did not arrive suddenly, it will necessarily take time to overcome. How to overcome that fear—as an individual and as a nation—is the subject of this book. *Freedom From Fear* provides a guide to shepherd Americans through the recovery process.

Step 1

Face the Mirror: Admit You Are an Addict

A twenty-seven-year-old patient recently terminated care and left my practice. He is highly intelligent, communicates well, and considers himself to be informed on all pandemic-related issues. He also suffers from a chronic anxiety disorder, one that he has been battling for over a decade. Although he had always respected my views about pandemic hysteria—despite voicing some disagreement with them—he found it intolerable that I did not wear a mask in my office while meeting with him.

Not surprisingly, he insisted on wearing a mask himself whenever he came to see me, believing it would protect him from getting sick. He was unable to rationally explain how my not wearing a mask could make him vulnerable to catching a virus that his mask was apparently protecting him from. He was one of the first in line to receive the drug that has been (incorrectly) called a vaccine, something that encouraged him to briefly leave his home on occasion. Once the "booster" drug advisory appeared, though, he once again retreated to the four walls of his apartment and refused to leave until he was eligible for an additional injection. I have no doubt this cycle will continue indefinitely for him. He is a fear addict.

He is not the only one.

The first step in conquering any addiction is to acknowledge it: You have been living in fear. And you have developed an addiction to it.

Americans have been terrorized by the government, the media, and corporations into fearing life. I explain in my first book, *United States of Fear*, how this process occurred, insidiously and covertly, not just in the past two years but over many decades. It accelerated rapidly in 2020, with the fear mongers using a Chinese virus as a pretext to spread a pandemic of fear throughout the nation. As the fear evolved into a chronic condition, millions of Americans became traumatized. They lost the ability to reason, they lost their relationships with family and friends, and they lost their education and jobs. They abandoned physical touch with other human beings, the acknowledgment of others in public, their sense of connectedness with people, and their feeling of purpose in life. In short, they replaced meaning with the empty, unsatisfying, and ultimately unattainable pursuit of "staying safe."

Like all addictions, fear addiction can be defined as a combination of loss of control and use despite harm. It all started innocently. Americans were told they were at risk and that they needed to be afraid. A temporary sacrifice by all was necessary to ensure everyone's safety. What began as an understandable, purposeful, defensive posture in early 2020, however, slowly transformed into an all-consuming and never-ending quest to satisfy the craving for reassurance and safety.

As with any mind-altering drug, the experience of fear initially provided a paradoxical relief, as it led to actions that felt protective, like mask-wearing and avoiding strangers. Businesses closed, and schools converted to remote learning. These steps gave people the illusion of being in control, of "doing something" about the problem. People also seemed to enjoy the suspension of normal routine and the retreat into a cocoon, insulated from the world with their partners and families. The government facilitated this process by controlling information and enacting a system of rewards and punishments: daily infection, hospitalization, and death bulletins; business and school closures; mask mandates; "social distancing" protocols; and "COVID relief" payments.

Not surprisingly, however, these temporary actions developed into a habit. Fear-driven behaviors eventually became reflexive, unconscious, and difficult to override. Like the physical release gained by smoking a cigarette, the initial relief from anxiety that the fear-driven behavior offered lost its effect over time, requiring greater and greater "doses" for the user to receive the same effect. This process of perpetual dose increase is called habituation. When one mask no longer offers adequate "protection," two become necessary. When one round of injections wears off after three months, a "booster" will solve the problem.

In concert with habituation, Americans also developed a dependency on fear. For an addict, dependency is the inability to stop using without suffering the discomfort of withdrawal, even when continued use causes personal injury. If the thought of returning to a life that does not revolve around fear produces anxiety, you have likely developed a dependency. Dependency represents a hurdle to overcoming addiction because the withdrawal it provokes can be terribly uncomfortable. Fear has become a drug, with all its accompanying damage.

A local fiction writer in her late sixties invited me to join her and her husband for dinner at an upscale restaurant in Beverly Hills over Christmas in 2021. She has led a rather impressive life, growing up in the Iranian capital of Tehran and fleeing to the U.S. during the Iranian Revolution, settling in the U.S. to write provocative stories set in the culture she left behind. She is well-educated and well-read, and speaks at least three languages. She is also living in fear.

Two nights before we were to meet, I received an email from her that read, "I have reserved a table on the terrace outdoors. I'd like to know if you have been vaccinated and boosted." I phoned her back right away and asked her why she cared. "Well, my husband and I have had three shots, but we've only recently begun to go out again, and we don't want to take any unnecessary risks." She then went on to explain that her husband had already been infected with the Wuhan virus in early 2020, recovered, and then went on to receive three injections anyway. "He has a heart condition, so he needs to protect himself," she said.

Despite her intelligence and education, she clearly had no understanding of basic immunology, natural immunity, or the known cardiac risks of the drug her husband had received not once but three times. I explained all this to her, as well as my decision to not take any of the shots, and she listened respectfully yet ultimately canceled the dinner reservation, saying: "Maybe we'll do it later… when it's safe."

For this woman, it will never be safe enough to return to normal life. Her irrational fear has hobbled her ability to live fully, locked her away in her home for nearly two years, and is now limiting her exposure only to people who have been injected with a drug that confers no immunity, no protection from catching disease, and no protection from spreading infection to others. She can attest to being afraid, but she has yet to acknowledge that she is addicted to fear, that her life is being controlled by it, and that she is suffering harm by not addressing it. Given her age, she may spend the rest of her life largely imprisoned in a cell of her own making, sacrificing the years that remain on the altar of safety.

As with alcoholics or any other type of addict, acknowledging an addiction to fear may be the most difficult step to take, but it is a necessary one. As I tell my patients, we must start with reality. If not, we will continue to live our lives through lies. Every subsequent step in the process of overcoming addiction relies on truth as a foundation for the work that must be done. Reality can only be sidestepped for so long, and then it must be faced. Why not face it head-on?

A middle-aged woman came to see me in my office in late fall 2021. She was wearing gloves, two masks, and a face shield. She told me that she worked for a high-profile executive at a well-known entertainment company in Hollywood. "Everyone is getting vaccinated, because that's what's expected where I work," she told me. "I don't want to take the vaccine, but I'm worried I may be forced to, or I'll lose my job."

I was confused. Covered in multiple layers of protective gear, the woman sitting in front of me was clearly terrified of catching the Wuhan virus. Why, then, was she so opposed to the shot? "I don't trust it. It hasn't been proven safe or effective," she said. "No one knows what the real side-effect risks are. I don't want it." She then went on to explain that despite her strong misgivings about the injectable drug, she was paralyzed by fear of catching the virus. "I know my behavior is irrational, bordering on obsessive-compulsive, and that it is handicapping my life," she admitted. "I'm anxious all the time, and wearing all this stuff calms me down. I know that at some point I need to stop, but I'm not ready to do it right now." She could acknowledge her fear addiction, as well as the harm it was causing her, but she had not yet decided to overcome it. Without the clear, expressed desire to relinquish the addiction, no further progress can be made.

What leads you to acknowledge your fear addiction and desire to let go of it is not important. Perhaps you have hit rock bottom—poor health, no friends, no job—and ending your life is not an option. You have no other choice at this point. More likely, though, you are simply weary. You have been living with the addiction for so long that the toll it has taken on you and those around you has far outstripped any possible benefit, real or imagined, that it once brought you. You are simply done. You have had enough. You have discovered that the life of an addict is lonely, empty, and unfulfilling.

At the beginning, you felt that you belonged to a virtuous, upstanding, caring group of people who were taking a significant threat to individual and public health seriously. Whether or not you have come to realize that you have been deceived, you no longer wish to participate in this all-consuming and utterly empty practice of worshipping the false god of safety. You are ready to leave the cult and sever ties with the guru. This is no longer the life you desire. What you want is freedom from fear, freedom from addiction, and the freedom to make non-fear-based decisions about how to live your life. You are ready to acknowledge your fear and leave it behind.

It is critical, though, that you come clean—no excuses or rationalizations. No "I may be scared, but I can stop any time," "I may be scared, but it isn't really a problem," or "I may be scared, but there are people much more scared than I am." This is the addict talking, desperately trying to protect himself from facing the truth of his addiction. Facing that truth may bring shame or embarrassment. It will certainly cause you to see yourself differently, and perhaps help you question other self-harming behaviors and choices. But it will also provide freedom—freedom from fear.

We are all afraid of something. We all suffer fear—rational and not. Many of us fear growing old or dying. Others fear losing their jobs. Some fear elevators, snakes, or airplane travel. Fear is part of the human condition. There is no way to eliminate all fear, nor would we want to. Fear provides information about potential risks we might consider avoiding, such as running through traffic to cross a busy intersection. It is not fear that needs to be conquered. It is the control and harm that fear addiction causes that must be faced honestly, if we are to take back our lives.

Look in the mirror and ask yourself, "Am I addicted to fear?" If the answer is yes, acknowledge the addiction and announce a sincere desire to overcome it.

Step 2

Don't Be a Sheep: Reject the Collective

For the past two years, sheep have been in vogue as symbols of mindless compliance—in cartoons, in memes, on T-shirts, and in videos. A large herd of sheep is seen making its way down a cobblestone street in the center of an old village, bleating, "Off to get another booster shot for something that hasn't worked twice already." Another group of hundreds, all wearing surgical masks, is standing at attention: "Staaaaay saaaaaaaafe." One sheep is standing alone, sporting a mask on his face and a giant syringe in his rear end. He simply says, "Baaaaaaah."

Sheep make an excellent metaphor for most Americans today, who are herdlike, docile, easily led, and more easily deceived. The main difference between sheep and contemporary Americans is that sheep actually feel safe in a herd. Try to find a group of grown Americans in an urban area relaxing together fewer than six feet apart, unmasked. A rare sighting.

In their defense, sheep—unlike actual Americans—have few tools to protect themselves with. They are easy prey for a host of predators, including wolves and aggressive dogs. They move slowly. They lack sharp teeth and claws. And they're not very bright. Their only hope for survival against attack is to band together in a herd and move as one unit. It also helps if they have an alert shepherd to ward off any impending attacks.

In contrast, Americans have an immense array of defensive tools and capabilities to protect themselves from harm. In addition to speed, agility, strength, and a concealed handgun, they can use their highly evolved brains to *think*. They can assess risk. They can research a new environment before they enter it. They can make use of the complementary skills and knowledge of others around them. Tragically, most of them have given up all these assets, driven by fear to sacrifice them on the altar of safety. They have joined a collective that promises protection from the wolf prowling nearby. This is the collective of M. Night Shyamalan's 2004 film *The Village*, in which the youth are infantilized and deceived by the adults in the town, who terrorize them with a fictitious monster living in the woods. These adults swear that anyone who fails to follow their mandate and who ventures beyond the village limits will be murdered. There is no actual evidence this monster exists, or that it has murdered in the past. Beyond a few nighttime sightings from a distance, there are only legends and the fear instilled in the children through the authority of the adults, who promise that they will be placing their lives at risk should they disobey the mandates.

One young woman begins to question the existence of the monster. Despite being blind, she comes to discover that there is no monster. It was invented by the older generation purely to control the children through fear, ostensibly to protect them from the dangers of life outside the village. Displaying tremendous courage, she separates from the collective and returns to the world outside, an urban environment full of danger and the unknown, to obtain life-saving medicine for a critically ill villager.

Ironically, the use of fear to isolate and "protect" the vulnerable puts everyone at greater risk. It wasn't until the collective in the film was successfully challenged that the real threat could be addressed and conquered. That threat was fear: fear of change, fear of violence, fear of death itself.

We are living in a village-like collective today in the United States. The main difference between Shyamalan's village and our own is that unlike the village elders in the movie, those who threaten us with monsters and mandates in today's America do not have our best interests at heart. This is the most important reason why we must all reject the collective, especially those who suffer from an addiction to fear.

The collective is not just a group. It is groupthink. It is like a mob, a mass of people who move and act as one without reflective thought. It disallows internal critique. It punishes dissent. The collective is not formed from a shared set of values. It is more akin to tribalism, by which individual differences are sacrificed to reinforce solidarity, with the purpose of preserving the survival of the tribe. Truth is not valued. Neither is compassion or justice. The invention of an enemy is often required to justify enforcing homogeneity of thought, appearance, and behavior. Acts of fealty to the tribe, however irrational or self-injurious, are demanded to maintain membership. Wearing masks has become a public act of fealty to the collective today. And just as primitive cultures adopted scarification to denote membership, today's collective requires injections, accompanied by a physical or electronic identifier.

Admittedly, joining the collective is a seductive option. When I was in high school, nearly one-third of the freshman class played football. Many of the students had little athletic skill, and fewer still had a passion for football. Most simply didn't know what to do, and gravitated toward football as the simplest answer to the question "What extracurricular activity should I join?" It was easy to be on the football team, at least during the first and second years. The team took all comers. And unless you repeatedly failed to show up for practice, you wouldn't get cut. Only an elite subgroup was inducted into the varsity team, but senior year was a long way off for a freshman. Why be concerned about the future? Being part of the team right out of the gate provided a sense of membership, identity, and meaning for the young, lost souls who had just entered high school with no idea of what they wanted to do with their lives.

Many Americans have joined today's collective for similar reasons. They lack meaning in their lives. They lack purpose. The collective offers a simple solution to the problem of self-definition: It tells you what to think and how to act, and in return, the group will give you an identity and a mission. There is even a uniform that serves to identify you as a member. You wear it on your face for all to see. It says, "I, too, am afraid."

While solitary addicts exist, most prefer to congregate in groups. Drunks attract other drunks. Heroin users attract other heroin users. They feel safe and protected drinking together in bars or shooting up together in derelict buildings because they have an understanding that no one within the group will call the others out for the harm caused by irresponsible drug use. There is an unspoken agreement among users that the reality of their lives will always be ignored and never challenged, to facilitate the addiction. This is why addicts always eventually separate themselves from their families and find new "families" in the addict community. Honest families challenge the addict by reflecting back to him, like a mirror, the ugly reality of his life. This is intolerable for the addict, who is always lying in one form or another—to himself, to others, to the world. For this reason, he seeks out a collective of other addicts equally at peace with devaluing truth, with twisting reality to meet their needs to maintain their addiction.

Conflict arises when an addict is confronted by someone who cares about him and who refuses to go along with the fantasy that what he is doing is in his best interests. Nicholas Cage's character struggled with this in the film *Leaving Las Vegas*—he chose to drink himself to death over several weeks in the company of a prostitute, a woman who was there only to do a job but slowly developed an attachment to him as a human being. Although she had promised to never tell him to stop drinking, she found it impossible to stay with him as he slowly disintegrated from the effects of the alcohol he was consuming nearly twenty-four hours a day. He demanded she join him in his fantasy that drinking himself to death was the only way out of a life defined by poor judgment, but witnessing the ongoing self-harm was simply too painful for her. His final days would have been spent more comfortably within a group of self-loathing alcoholics. That would, of course, have deprived the film of its primary conflict: the addict versus the one who loves and pities him. When you are an addict, you are destined to lead a lonely and isolated life, unless you find a group of other addicts who will join you in forming a collective dedicated to subverting reality.

The benefits of rejecting the collective don't always appear immediately. In fact, you should expect your tribe to make every effort to keep you within the group. You will be criticized, mocked, shamed, and ostracized. I certainly was when I published a critique of lockdowns in April 2020, spoke out against school closures in May 2020, and began giving interviews on mass delusional psychosis in the fall. The attacks were swift in coming, from both the public and a subset of my family, friends, and patients: "You realize that you are in the minority." "Why do all the others I know disagree with you?" "You're a quack—you should lose your license." These are some of the milder reactions to my unapologetic departure from the collective view on lockdowns. To all of these criticisms, I responded in the same way: I would rather be right than be in the majority.

The benefits came later. As rigid or brainwashed patients disavowed me, and as well-meaning but weak family members and friends distanced themselves, a new space opened up filled with highly motivated and curious patients, as well as independent-minded, courageous colleagues and friends. The only universally shared quality among every fear addict I have encountered is a total absence of curiosity. This, more than anything, primes them for herdlike nonthinking and leaves them vulnerable to fear-based predation. I have never met a curious sheep.

Although I was never afraid, much less addicted to fear, I discovered that I had been investing much of my professional and personal energy in maintaining relationships with people who simply were uninterested in or unable to participate in a meaningful dyad. They preferred the safety of the collective to the risky unknowns of freedom and personal accountability. They would rather be wrong than be in the minority. They chose to maintain a fantasy life within the collective because they could not conceive the possibility that leaving it would offer them the opportunity of membership in a much more nourishing and powerful group of independent and curious thinkers. Their fear of finding themselves alone and isolated overwhelmed any desire to be free. They preferred the lie that the collective would take care of them over the truth that only by leaving the collective would they ever be truly free.

Sometimes the benefits of leaving the collective do arrive immediately. Three years ago, I was involved in a life-threatening car accident. Driving home to Los Angeles from San Diego on the freeway, my car was struck by a pickup truck at seventy miles per hour. My car spun out of control, crossed five lanes of traffic, and hit the divider facing the opposite direction—into oncoming traffic. Multiple airbags deployed, and windows shattered. When the car came to rest, it took me a few seconds to realize that I was still alive. The paramedics who arrived minutes later, having seen the condition of the car, couldn't believe that I was unharmed, much less that I had been able to get out of the car and walk without assistance to a safe area. What surprised me the most was how calm I felt the moment I knew I had survived without serious injury. A switch had been flipped in my brain, and for several months I found myself incapable of wasting time on anything that I deemed unimportant.

One important task I had to complete was the purchase of a new car. I had never owned one before. I had always driven a used car, as I could never afford a new one, being a perpetual student without a salary. Buying a new car, though, is time-consuming. All my life, I had heard stories of people visiting dealerships with a plan to make a quick purchase and leave, only to find themselves held hostage by a disreputable salesman who refused to negotiate in good faith, frequently leaving the office to speak with his manager and then returning with new terms to haggle over. The process often dragged on for hours until the new-car buyer was so worn down that he simply accepted the deal that was on the table—often one not in his favor—just to get the process over with. Since my accident, I felt I had no time to waste on this form of theater, and I resolved to find another way.

After deciding on the make and model of car I wanted, I emailed several dealers nearby, letting them know I was interested in purchasing a car. I asked them to make me an offer. Once I received their responses, I shared the best offer with the rest of the group. This produced even better offers. After several rounds, it became clear I was approaching the best possible offer. I took it and informed the salesman I would not be coming to the dealership to complete any paperwork. He would deliver the car to my home, paperwork prefilled, and I would simply sign it and take the keys. He agreed. We found a time that worked for me, and he showed up with the car, went over the operation of the vehicle, had me sign a couple of completed forms, handed me the keys, and left. I received a much better offer than I ever could have by visiting the dealership in person, saved hours of time and energy, and never had to leave my house.

The collective expects you to spend many hours, often over several days, haggling with a recalcitrant salesman on-site where he works, to buy a new car. You have other options. These options may not be advertised by the dealer, because they don't favor him. You may feel uncomfortable or afraid of considering them. "It's just not the way it's done...everyone else is going to the dealer in person, so that must be the right way of doing things." This thinking drives new-car purchases just as it drives adherence to mandates to wear masks or stay six feet apart from others. It's part of a groupthink that benefits only the party in power at the expense of the individual. It takes courage to announce you will not be going along with it. That action does not need to be mean, rude, or violent. It simply needs to be firm and assertive. It needs to announce that you are standing up for yourself, where it matters, regardless of the expectations of the collective.

The dean of my medical school wore a button on his coat that read, "Because this is the way we've always done it," with a thick red line through the words. He refused to be part of the collective. Although he was always respectful, he asked questions and challenged orthodoxy. He knew that simply accepting what we are told to do, without pausing to think about it, leads to injury and loss of life. It also invites the corrupt to take advantage of the compliant for their own benefit. Even twenty years ago medicine operated much like a collective. Today it operates only as a collective. Physicians have become addicted to fear as well, through coercion and intimidation. They no longer operate autonomously. They no longer value ethical practice or honor "do no harm." Witness their nearly universal refusal to offer any treatment to those infected with the Wuhan virus. They would rather see patients die than risk challenging the collective ideology that argues for the first time in medical history that we have no way of treating a respiratory infection other than with an injection of an unproven "vaccine." Medical doctors now work as a collective, to the detriment of their patients and their profession.

Whether a doctor, a teacher, a mother, or a student, you must leave the collective to overcome your fear. Rejecting fear addiction requires rejecting the group. If you do not leave it, you can never develop protection from the undue influence of the herd. Rejecting the collective will also protect you from relapse from the fear addiction, as you challenge yourself to develop strength on your own rather than using the false support of the group as a crutch. By cultivating curiosity toward different ideas and opinions, contemporary events, and other people, you discover that you not only do not need the collective, but that being part of it actually weakens your character and prevents you from fulfilling your potential.

Reject the collective. Separate from the herd.

Step 3

Live in the Real World: Choose Reality Over Fantasy

You have developed a fear of bugs. You see them everywhere, especially inside your home. It's become so bad that you've covered the walls, floors, and ceiling with aluminum foil to keep them out. You rarely leave the house now. Your girlfriend has joined you in your fear, agreeing to move in with you so that you can join forces in combatting the infestation. The bugs are hiding everywhere, even in your teeth, which you begin to manually extract one by one with a pair of pliers for immediate inspection under a magnifying lens. Eventually, no one comes in or out of the house. You nail shut all the doors and windows. Nothing you do can keep them out, however. They have taken over, and there seems to be no way to protect yourself. You have run out of options. Self-immolation appears to be your only way out. You douse yourself and your girlfriend with gasoline and light a match. That will show them.

This is the fantasy described in the 2006 movie *Bug*. The characters played by Ashley Judd and Harry Connick

Jr. suffer from delusional parasitosis—a fear of bugs. The delusional fear begins with the man, who also suffers from PTSD. His girlfriend, seemingly rational at the beginning of the film, develops a *folie à deux* with him and begins to accept his fear as real. She follows his lead in the decontamination procedures, and the two sequester themselves within his house, too frightened to go outside. By the end, their fears have completely overtaken them, to the point that they choose death over confronting reality.

What happens when a shared fear fantasy between two people becomes shared throughout a whole society? Every individual suffers. Self-deception leads to self-harm. Fantasy rather than reality begins to guide all decision-making. Imagined threats replace real threats, and productive life grinds to a halt. Fantasies based on fear and driven by paranoia wind up crippling both the individual and the collective.

A sixty-five-year-old woman came to see me for an evaluation for anxiety. She was spraying her hands with sanitizer when I met her in the waiting room. She was wearing two masks. I invited her to take them off, which she did only reluctantly. After sitting down in my office, she asked me, "Have you been vaccinated?" When I told her I had not and never would receive the mRNA injection, her eyes filled with terror, she stood up, and then she slowly backed into the wall behind her, replacing both masks on her face. She scowled at me and said, "You probably voted for Trump."

I looked at her and said, "I don't know what Donald Trump has to do with this, but I am curious about something: You believe these shots are protective, don't you?" She nodded vigorously. "So then why does it matter to you if I've had them?" A full minute of silence passed. She had nothing to say. I looked directly into her eyes and said, "You aren't just anxious. You are suffering from an addiction to fear." She chastised me for "criticizing" her and suggested that I "shouldn't be saying that sort of thing." I countered that, in truth, it was my *responsibility* to tell her, because part of my job is to challenge patients when they engage in self-harm. "You are harming yourself with your addiction," I told her. "And I will help you with it if you are ready to work on it." She kept both her masks on but did stop arguing with me, and eagerly took my advice on how to begin the process of overcoming her fear.

I can predict how much a patient will improve in treatment by how willing he is to accept reality. Reality is a starting point. That's why I often tell a new patient that for us to work together, we both must share the same reality. In fact, my responsibility as a treater is to honor reality regardless of what mental world the patient inhabits. This can lead to a great deal of distress for the patient, depending on how far away from reality he lies and how strongly he resists moving toward it When a new patient shows me that he is not yet even aware he is living in a fantasy, I know we have preparatory work to do before we can begin collaborating on how to work on the real external problems.

A mother who comes to me and says, "I'm suffering because I cannot allow my son to walk to school. If I do, he'll be kidnapped," occupies a very different world than the mother who says, "I'm suffering because I *imagine* he'll be kidnapped." The second woman is living in reality but is tormented by her paranoia. The first is simply paranoid. Both cases are treatable, but almost certainly the first woman has a poorer prognosis. She hasn't yet acknowledged that the source of her suffering isn't the external world—it lies inside her. Until she realizes that she will continue to suffocate her son and enable her own self-harm. She may even alienate other mothers in the neighborhood if she advocates that they, too, "protect" their children by prohibiting them from walking to school. Of course, if all mothers in the neighborhood feared that their children would be kidnapped, this mother's fantasy would be reinforced. She would be part of a collective. Until she chose to reject the collective, it would be impossible for her to ever leave her addiction behind because the group pressure to maintain it would overwhelm any therapeutic intervention.

I once worked with an attractive woman in her early thirties whose primary complaint was that she had been forced to leave every professional position she had ever held due to sexual harassment. "Wherever I work, men come on to me—colleagues and bosses—and I have to go," she told me. As I got to know her better, I learned that she had felt unloved and abandoned by her father since she was a little girl. After several months of working with her in therapy four days a week, I suggested that it was possible she had instigated the sexualization of her professional relationships due to an unconscious desire to obtain her father's love through the attention of her colleagues and bosses. She rejected this possibility entirely, despite acting out that very behavior with me in the office. She frequently regressed and spoke with me as if she were a girl trying to please her father. Eventually, she left treatment after accusing me of trying to seduce her. She couldn't choose reality over fantasy. It would have been too humiliating for her.

This is the challenge of living in the real world rather than in a fantasy. It's harder. It requires more of you: accountability, maturity, and humility. It gets in the way of using other people and the world at large as excuses for your failures and lack of goal attainment. Unlike fantasies, where good and evil are clearly defined, real life is messy. Good people disappoint, sometimes due to nothing other than their own limitations. The love you feel you deserve to receive from your parents may never arrive. You will inevitably lose people you care about to accidents and illness, and you won't always be prepared to lose them.

Not every bad outcome has a villain. Generating fantasies that there is one will not ease the suffering—just the opposite, in fact. It will deprive you of any hope that you will act with agency in your life. It will guarantee that you will become a victim as well as a prisoner to your own fear. You will become miserable and ungrateful, angry and cynical. Your impotence toward participation in the real world will deprive you of achieving your potential as a unique human being. Living in a fantasy has profound real-world consequences.

While living in Geneva, Switzerland, after graduating high school, I met a man in his early forties who had started dating a woman in her twenties. They soon moved in together, she quit her job, and he began supporting her financially as she began a multi-year academic program to prepare for admission to medical school. I liked both of them and enjoyed their company. I was struck, though, by the unequal investment in the relationship. He seemed to be enthralled with her and hoped to marry her. Her passion, though, appeared to be the study of medicine. His family became concerned that perhaps she was simply using him to pay her way until she graduated, and they warned him of the possibility. He brushed off their concerns as nothing more than an expression of jealousy toward an older man enjoying the company of a much younger woman.

After a year, I returned to the United States but stayed in touch with him. Eventually, his girlfriend graduated medical school and promptly left him for a younger man. He was devastated. To this day, he is not married and cannot trust women. Had he accepted the reality of the transactional nature of his relationship with this younger woman, he could have decided with eyes open whether to stay in the relationship. He chose instead to live in a fantasy, a fantasy that broke him when she ultimately left him.

I don't mean to imply that fantasies are always bad. They serve a useful purpose. Fantasies provide a creative outlet, as well as a forum or workspace for play. Movies are often based on fantasies. So are games: Buying up all the high-end properties in a Monopoly game can make you feel rich and powerful for an hour or two. When little boys play cowboys and Indians, they are taking on temporary roles in a battlefield fantasy (not acting out cultural appropriation, colonialism, or racism, as contemporary critics often charge). When little girls prepare mud cakes in the yard, they are exploring a fantasy of using ingredients to prepare food.

Some adults engage in sexual fantasies with their partners using role-play to explore taboos and fetishes, such as dominance and submission, the infliction of physical pain or humiliation, and even rape. Many of these fantasies, were they performed in reality and without consent, would be seen as acts of infidelity, abuse, or criminality. In the context of a consensual relationship, though, they can strengthen the couple's bond, building trust and allowing exploration of hidden areas of desire. When sexual fantasies are not shared openly by someone in a couple, on the other hand, they are more likely to be acted out outside the relationship without the partner's knowledge or consent. Fantasies serve a necessary role for both children and adults. They allow human beings to be creative and to play without incurring the risks of acting in the real world.

Fear-driven fantasies, in contrast to creative fantasies, block growth and development. A child who fears serious injury by falling off his bike never learns how to ride one. Later, if he fears being eaten by sharks in the ocean or having his foot caught in the drain in a pool, he never learns to swim. In junior high school, if he fears being socially ostracized for flubbing a speech in front of his classmates, he declines all public speaking opportunities. If he fears being rejected by a girl, he never asks one out. Somehow he manages to get married but later divorces, and he fears his next marriage will turn out the same way. So he remains alone for the rest of his life. In every case, his fears have impeded him from attaining his full potential.

I have met someone with each of the fears described above. While it's certainly possible to live a full life without ever learning how to swim or participate in public speaking, fear-driven fantasies tend not to occur in isolation. One gives birth to another, and they multiply. Fear provides an excuse to avoid taking risks, and a life devoid of risk-taking is not a life well-lived. The goal of life is not to live safely—it is to live fully. Every fear-driven fantasy one embraces circumscribes that fullness, limiting it and removing an area of potential exploration.

Limitations can be self-imposed through fear in a number of ways. My grandfather believed that once he had earned a certain amount of money, any additional dollar received would trigger a total confiscation of all his earnings. To protect himself—to keep himself financially safe—he simply stopped earning money once he approached that self-imposed limit. He continued to work but would not accept payment for his services. He had artificially capped his economic growth. I have female patients who fear the desire of men, so they intentionally gain weight and stop grooming. As male attention wanes, they initially take comfort in feeling unseen. Later, though, their loneliness leads to depression when they cannot initiate or maintain an intimate relationship. A male graduate student in my practice feared he would fail if he were to be hired by a prestigious investment firm after completing his MBA. He sabotaged his interviews and accepted a less competitive job offer so that there was no chance he would not be successful. Now he complains regularly that his classmates are "doing so well" in their jobs at the very firms he interviewed with two years ago.

In every one of the examples above, it was not the environment that placed these individuals at risk—it was an internal fear fantasy. They were terrorized by their inner world, not the world outside.

Inner fear fantasies drive fantasy solutions, while real-world fears drive real solutions. This is why living in a fantasy world cannot generate tools that solve actual problems. If an overweight diabetic who does not exercise becomes captive to fear of a respiratory virus from China, his focus becomes finding a fantasy solution to this new threat. Rather than taking stock of his situation holistically and acknowledging that his obesity and preexisting medical condition are placing him at risk of an early demise, he pursues the opposite of what would increase his chance of survival: He locks himself in his apartment, sits in front of his computer, and orders takeout. Social isolation, immobility, and an unhealthy diet now conspire to further shorten his lifespan. When he does go out, he "protects" himself with an "amulet"—a mask—believing that this alone will guarantee him everlasting life. He responds to his inner fear by pursuing a fantasy solution rather than confronting the real threat to his health. The latter would require actual work and honest engagement with the outside world. He isn't ready to do that.

I frequently see patients refusing to live in reality who displace their real fears onto fantasy fears to avoid doing the work necessary to improve their lives. They simply do not want to interact honestly with reality, so they generate fantasies that serve as obstacles to their reentry into real life. A middle-aged gay man in my practice had been estranged from his family for decades, yet he blamed all his contemporary relationship problems on Donald Trump, who he was convinced was a homophobic racist. When he learned that I had spoken in Washington, D.C., with a group of physicians whom President Trump had publicly supported on Twitter, he abruptly terminated treatment, citing my affiliation with the offensive group lauded by a homophobic and racist president. I don't believe he has much chance of improving his relationships as long as he sees Trump as the real threat, rather than unresolved conflicts with his biological family.

Living in reality builds one's capacity to tolerate fear in general. Through successful confrontation with reality, one's confidence grows to be able to handle greater threats. One also develops character by repeatedly testing one's capacities in real-world applications. Fantasy does not do this and often, in fact, gets in the way. Many students I went to college with at the University of California, Berkeley, believed that when they were high on marijuana, their creative minds were unleashed and they wrote better papers. During their period of intoxication, they genuinely felt masterful in their ability to express complex thoughts elegantly, completing entire term papers over the course of an evening.

The problem was that under more sober scrutiny, what they had written revealed itself to be a jumble of disconnected and poorly developed thoughts lacking objective support. Those who could be honest with themselves recognized the work product as a farce, began again, and never attempted to complete future assignments within a cloud of smoke. Others refused to allow reality to judge them, deferring that to their professors, whom they could then accuse of being closed-minded once the paper was returned with a poor grade. After I spent several years seeing addicts in residential treatment centers, it became clear to me that regular drug use always precludes a life lived in reality and inevitably leads to a developmental arrest. One must confront reality in order to grow.

For a time, I followed mixed martial arts. The sport today bears no resemblance to what occurred in 1993 during the first Ultimate Fighting Championship (UFC). Back then, many fighters came from schools that had trained students only in artificial settings, so these fighters had never tested their skills in real combat. They had been training in a fantasy world and were confronted with reality the moment they entered the ring to face off against an opponent who had known and inflicted real violence. In a matter of hours, the reality of a no-holds-barred fight revealed which fighting techniques actually worked and which were fun to watch in a simulated fight but were of limited effectiveness against a determined and truly well-trained opponent. When a Dutch kickboxer kicked a four-hundred-pound Sumo wrestler in the face, knocking out three of his teeth (one landed underneath the announcer's table, and the two others became embedded in the kickboxer's foot), all remaining fantasy was dispelled. Reality won, and professional fighting was changed forever.

Fear addiction and living in the real world cannot coexist. They are like oil and water. The fantasies that maintain the addiction are based on lies. One can certainly construct an artificial world to contain one's lies, but it remains just as false as the fantasies it supports. The greatest fantasy of all is that of one's own immortality. The understandable fear of death is nearly ubiquitous precisely because death is inevitable.

I believe that many human beings in well-developed nations today have so distanced themselves from the natural cycle of life and death that the arrival of even a relatively innocuous virus has terrified them because it reminds them of their own mortality. Many quickly and earnestly adopted ridiculous, superstitious measures such as home sequestration, antisocial distancing, overzealous sanitation procedures, and mask-wearing in a fervent yet ultimately hopeless effort to root out the possibility that they, too, will eventually die. This practice developed into an obsession, culminating in addiction.

If this describes you, know that you are not alone. Know also that your fantasy of cheating death is based on a lie. More important, know that by continuing to live that lie, you are, ironically, turning your back on the life you have to live right now. This is the ultimate travesty—by denying death, you are preventing life.

How do you live in the real world rather than in a fantasy world? First, you must be honest with yourself and acknowledge that you have been making up stories to make yourself temporarily comfortable so that you can avoid facing realities that produce discomfort. If you don't know what those stories are—if you are unable to distinguish between fantasy and reality—then you need to ask someone you trust to help you. Ask this person, "Where am I lying to myself? What do you see that I don't, especially when it comes to areas of life that are challenging? What am I avoiding?" A true friend (or an experienced therapist) should be able to assist you in answering these questions.

There is no point in focusing only on your weaknesses, but a sincere quest for honesty mixed with compassion can only strengthen your character and expand your freedom. This does require courage, but luckily courage is simply a choice. Making the choice to be courageous is the only thing that separates the courageous from the cowardly.

Second, ask yourself whom you admire for their strength, courage, and sincerity. Ask those individuals how they manage to maintain a life grounded in reality that rejects lies and self-deception. Each person will offer you a different answer and a unique tool that you may find useful: meditation, prayer, competitive fitness, music and other forms of creative expression, caring for a child or parent. Self-reflection and full engagement with a project or an activity that truly matters to you can help reveal and challenge unhelpful, fear-based fantasies that lead to self-limiting habits and a constrained life ruled by doubt, obsessing over risk, and paranoia. You can know when you are surrounding yourself with others who are living a fantasy life because you can observe an absence of growth. Those who live in reality are always growing. Seek them out and ask for their help. You may be surprised by the response.

Live in the real world. Choose reality over fantasy.

Step 4

Reject Narcissism: Your Fear Doesn't Matter to Society

As I was leaving the gym one day, I passed by the front desk, manned by a young woman I know personally. I overheard a masked gym member telling her, "I really like your mask." The member had no idea that the girl behind the desk hated wearing a mask and only did so because she was forced to by her employer, who is afraid one of the members will become terrified at the sight of an unmasked human face and file a complaint with the city health department.

I stopped, turned to the woman who had made the comment, and said, "I really like her *face*. Unfortunately, she rarely gets to show it to anyone now because of fearful people like you who have fetishized face diapers and bullied everyone around you into behaving as if they are just as afraid as you are." Her jaw dropped and a long period of silence ensued. She had no response.

That woman is a fear addict and a narcissist. She praises others for mirroring her own illness, with no understanding of how coercion is driving others to resemble her, at least at the behavioral level. When confronted with reality, she became paralyzed. Her narcissistic shell had been punctured.

A banner popularized in 2020 reads, "My freedom doesn't end where your fear begins." Of all the slogans birthed as a challenge to the government's response to the pandemic, this one is my favorite. Not only does it defend the sanctity of freedom, a core American value that has been nearly lost as the government has intruded into every aspect of our lives, but it also puts narcissism in its place. Addiction thrives on narcissism. Those who are addicted to fear believe their fear should dictate how others live. Nothing could be further from the truth. Their fear is utterly irrelevant to society. It is for them to manage, not to inflict on those around them.

Several patients recently left my practice because they couldn't tolerate my refusal to wear a mask in the office. One young man in his mid-twenties insisted on wearing his at every visit. He suffered from an anxiety disorder, not surprisingly. When he asked me why I wasn't wearing a mask, I replied honestly, "Because I find them dirty, dehumanizing, and dangerous. Additionally, they offer no measurable protection against infection." He was infuriated that I would not agree with him, not join him in his paranoia. I never ordered *him* to take his mask off, although I did invite him to. Yet he felt entitled to order *me* to put one on.

When I pointed out that his worship of the mask and the protection it conferred on him should be unaffected by any choice I made for myself, he suffered a narcissistic injury. In his eyes, I had actually harmed him by choosing to display a different view through my behavior. This is a childish, primitive, unevolved emotional position that adults have historically refused to countenance in anyone beyond the age of kindergarten. Narcissism, though, has recently developed into a virtue for many urban Americans. It is not. In adults, it can develop into a personality disorder.

On any given day, up to ten thousand Americans are recovering from chemotherapy, whole-body irradiation, or another invasive medical procedure that compromises the body's ability to fight off infection. Have they ever demanded, as a group, that everyone else living in the United States stay at home most of the time and wear masks when they go outside? These people know that they are particularly vulnerable to infection due to their medical condition, so they take precautions to keep themselves safe. They do not inflict their own liabilities—which are real, not imaginary—onto the broader population. To do so would be an act of profound narcissism. For over two years, this is exactly what those suffering from fear addiction have done.

In this, of course, they have been supported and encouraged by a loud chorus of irrational and irresponsible fearmongers in the press, the public health profession, and the government. So it isn't entirely their fault. But it is their problem—and ours.

While growing up, I celebrated Christmas with my extended family and opened presents on Christmas Eve at my grandparents' house. Everyone left their presents around a Christmas tree in the living room when they arrived, and we opened them after dinner. My sister and I were the family's only children at the time, so we received presents from everyone. One year we found an enormous wrapped gift that we were invited to open—it was a miniature pool table designed for children. Today I could carry it with one arm, but at the time it took up more space in the room than I did. Next Christmas, I slipped away from dinner early to examine the presents waiting to be opened. I saw another large box and assumed it was meant for me. Just like the previous year! I began to unwrap it before one of the adults saw what I was doing, came over to me, and said, "This isn't for you—it's for your grandparents." It was an air conditioner. Everyone in the family had pitched in to purchase it. I remember the embarrassment I felt at falsely assuming that the biggest present in the room belonged to me, just as it had the previous year. It was a reminder that although all the adults paid extra attention to me and my sister, Christmas wasn't about only us. It was about everyone in the family. I wasn't the most important person in the room.

Everyone is born a narcissist. This is not a bad thing. In fact, it is necessary for human survival. Babies live in an omnipotent fantasy in which they occupy the center of the universe, with everything and everyone revolving around them. Their view of the world is similar to that of all people on Earth before the 1500s, when Copernicus proposed what is known as the heliocentric model—that the earth revolves around the sun rather than the earth's being at the center of the universe. Until then, it had been largely assumed that the earth was located in the middle of everything. This assumption was based not on science or any mathematical calculation. It derived from a psychological stance common to all human beings—that they, and the planet they live on, must be the most important things anywhere. It simply did not occur to people before Copernicus that there could be any other planetary orientation. The earth's central position in the cosmos followed directly from the narcissistic position of its inhabitants: "I feel important, so I must be."

Babies have simple needs: warmth, nourishment, and cleaning. These needs are taken care of by mothers, who encourage babies' natural and instinctive narcissism by responding to their needs twenty-four hours a day, despite tremendous disruption to their own emotional well-being, including in their sleep, physical health, and marital relationship. A mother's own needs take a backseat once a baby is born so that the baby receives every ounce of the mother's attention. This maternal preoccupation, as the English pediatrician and psychoanalyst Donald Winnicott describes it, allows the mother to develop a sensitivity to her baby's needs that reassures the baby he will not be abandoned.

Gratification of the baby's narcissism is a psychological necessity for the baby at the beginning of his life, as he cannot physically meet his own needs. His mother's maternal preoccupation protects him from this devastating reality—that he is helpless—until he develops the psychological strength to accept his limitations. At this point, mother and baby can begin to separate, and both can return to meeting their respective needs on their own. At some point, the baby learns there are other human beings in his mother's life, and that he is only one of many who orbit around her. He is not the center of the universe, and she does not revolve around him. This is how normal human development proceeds.

One's egocentrism as a baby is a healthy expression of narcissism. As one gets older, though, clinging to an exaggerated focus on the self and its importance can be pathologic. In America today, unhealthy narcissism is driving the normalization of unique personal pronouns, transgenderism, and racial identity. This is all founded on a lie: How you view or express yourself physically, sexually, and grammatically does not matter to anyone else. In other words, these are private struggles that do not concern the general public. Pretending that they do—and should—is a purely narcissistic display reminiscent of an infant's worldview, one that elevates the importance of the self above all else and demands that this delusion be acknowledged and supported by society at large. This is not something to be proud of. It is embarrassing and should provoke some deep reflection on where things went wrong.

To a large degree, the persistence of narcissism in older children, adolescents, and young adults today stems from a lack or weakness of identity. At their core, narcissists are not full of themselves—they are empty. They have not developed an identity, so they seek to create an artificial one by taking on arbitrary, meaningless pseudo identities. It's like playing dress-up, trying on different outfits to cover your nakedness until you come to believe that you truly are what you wear.

Adults encourage this. Teachers now call their students by whatever name (or pronoun) the children wish. Coaches provide trophies for participation rather than for winning. In some places, offering a trophy to the winner is now banned because if there is a winner, then there must be a loser. We can't have that—everyone must be a winner. When I played soccer as a child, one of my coaches gave out a trophy for "most improved." I remember feeling jealous of the boy who received it until I learned that "most improved" meant you were not a good player to begin with. Thanks to that discovery, I became skeptical of trophies long before the idea of a participation trophy even existed.

I see parents today cooking separate meals for each child in the family so that everyone's preferences can be honored. What message is this sending to children? It's telling them that their subjective experiences, feelings, and desires are the most important things in the world and that they deserve to be catered to. This does not produce strong, resilient adults. It cultivates weakness, selfishness, and emotional fragility. It produces adults who believe that their fear should be respected and that *feeling* safe is something to strive for, even worthy of admiration.

The concept of "safe spaces" at universities has been widely mocked, and rightly so. Rather than encourage students to challenge themselves by confronting uncomfortable ideas, staffers perversely elevate their students' emotional states to a position of primacy above all else, sacrificing any possibility of growth and development. They infantilize their students, placing them in cribs with stuffed animals and sweets rather than allowing them to tolerate the temporary discomfort necessary to define an adult identity. They lie to them by saying that feelings should determine actions and that discomfort defines morality. These adults are hobbling an entire generation by colluding with the narcissistic tendency found in every child to view himself as the center of the universe and his feelings as the arbiter of right and wrong. This is as foolish as allowing an eight-year-old to decide what he eats for dinner every night.

What does all of this lead to? Americans of all ages are now under the false impression that their fear is meaningful to others and that it should be accommodated and catered to. They believe that public policy should be guided by the level of ambient fear within their community. Individual and group fears now drive the decisions of those in power. The fear addict lives in a narcissistic fantasy that his fear should be honored and that others should go out of their way to make him feel comfortable; the concept of individual liberty is subsumed by his subjective experience of fear. This is unhealthy, destructive, and ultimately unsustainable at both the individual and societal level.

Beneath the hard exterior of the narcissist, there is an emptiness. There is a lack of identity and, often, meaning. When fear is not confronted but instead validated by society, the individual comes to believe that his fear is good and virtuous—that his fear *matters* to society. Fear becomes his *raison d'être*, substituting for a hollowness inside himself. Just as low-level airline employees can become petty tyrants when granted the power to deprive paying customers of access to the plane when they refuse to hide their faces, those with a weak self-definition can embrace fear as their core identity when given a green light by society. This is self-deception, however. You must understand that your fear does not matter to anyone but you and other fear addicts with a vested interest in normalizing fear. If everyone is injecting heroin, the stigma of addiction is removed.

Encouraging narcissism can only harm the individual and society. The announcement of a crisis does not justify ennobling fear. Whenever anyone—child or adult—is praised for acting out his addiction, the illness is simply reinforced. When an *LA Times* columnist writes, "My sixth-grader may never give up her mask. If only adults could be this grown-up," she is encouraging her daughter to define her virtue by her display of commitment to fear.

I have banned masks for all children in my practice. I refuse to allow my patients to believe that their fear matters to me. They are welcome to talk about their fear, and we will discuss strategies to contain it—and to act in spite of it—but children are not welcome to wear a symbol of it on their faces. As adults, we have a responsibility to model courage for children, even if we feel afraid ourselves. Fear can never become an identity, lest it become an addiction.

What should you do if your identity has become wrapped up in fear, and you feel that your fear matters to society? The first step is to understand that this is the result of a shallow or fragile inner self. Someone who has developed an identity through years of facing the world head-on and grappling with the messiness of life does not allow fear to determine his behavior, and he certainly does not expect others to acknowledge his fear and praise him for it, much less conform their own behavior to his fear.

Perhaps you were brought up in a household where your parents didn't allow you to explore the world without sanitizing your experience—ensuring you would never experience pain, failure, or disappointment. You may never have had the opportunity to grow your resilience and confidence by taking risks, falling down, and then getting up again. Maybe you interpreted your parents' overprotection as proof that you just don't have what it takes to survive on your own. This is a common outcome with children who are not allowed to separate from their mother after one or two years of life. Some mothers find themselves unable to leave their state of maternal preoccupation and continue to focus so heavily on their child that the child never develops a strong individual identity. In addition, he continues to see himself as the center of attention—because that is how his mother relates to him—and begins to believe that his own feelings are what determine reality.

This problem cannot be solved in a day. It takes years to develop the problem and substantial therapeutic work to overcome it. There are steps you can take, though, that can at least send you in the right direction.

First, you must disavow fear as a virtue. It is nothing of the sort. Fear is simply information, often inaccurate information, that you can accept or reject as you make your own decisions on how to act. Feelings are not values. You cannot always decide what to feel, but you can decide what values to hold. By choosing to value courage, for example, you are placing your own ego at risk—a powerful stance against narcissism. If you then act courageously, your behavior will redefine you as someone who is fearless and less focused on protecting yourself from inconvenience, discomfort, or negative feelings than on pursuing your higher values. By directing your focus externally, thinking of how to meet others' needs rather than your own, you will increase your experience of gratitude, a prerequisite for happiness. Happiness does not exist in an ingrate. Gratitude and narcissism are essentially mutually incompatible.

As you continue to act in concert with your values, regardless of how you are feeling in the moment—sad, tired, fearful, resentful—you will come to understand that your true power lies in acting the way you know you should despite your current emotional state. You will have taken the reins and learned how to guide the horse, rather than allowing the horse to take you wherever he feels like going.

This is what the ancients meant by *virtue,* and it was taught as a practice for centuries throughout the Greco-Roman world. In the Stoic philosophy, it means not succumbing to your natural impulses but mastering and guiding them to their proper human ends. There is much wisdom in this ancient school of thought.

The discovery of fulfilling your potential will forever change the way you view yourself. No longer will you be controlled by fear and defined by it. You will be repulsed by the very idea of fear addiction, and you will certainly no longer feel proud of it. Rather than wearing fear as a badge of honor, pointing to it with every new encounter, your focus will become fulfilling your unique mission in life. Attention-seeking, controlling, and judgmental behaviors—all signs of a weak self-identity—will lose their grip on you. They will seem petty and inconsequential as the canvas of your life expands to include much more important goals, now that you no longer have to invest so much energy in protecting your former fragile self. It will no longer matter to you that you don't matter in the grander scheme of things; paradoxically, that recognition will allow you to matter more to others. Others will genuinely value your contributions, which will be heartfelt and honest. Those contributions no longer will be the desperate machinations of an infant in an adult body, constantly striving to find proof that he will not be abandoned. This is the road from narcissism to psychological health.

My work with drug addicts has always been challenging, for a variety of reasons. One reason is that they are always dishonest. You must constantly lie to yourself in order to maintain an addiction, and that leads to lying to others. Lying is the mechanism used to avoid reality. Another challenge with addicts is that they are often narcissistically preoccupied. They believe that their problems are more important than anyone else's, and they use that false belief to rationalize the harm they cause themselves and others.

This is no different in those who are addicted to fear. They justify their fear-driven behaviors by elevating their own experience above that of strangers, friends, and family. When challenged, they blurt out something about "my truth," as if that ends the argument. Next, they attack the virtue of whoever is holding them accountable for their misguided fear-driven behavior; their mindset is "You are selfish—you don't care about other people because you won't agree to cower in fear with me." Fear addicts frequently virtue-signal or invoke the authority of the collective as a way to deflect attention from their own inadequacies as less-than-fully-formed adults.

I completed a rotation in anesthesia pain medicine in medical school. Most of the patients were addicted to opiates. They would come into the outpatient hospital clinic once every ninety days for a refill of their pain medication. Every time they were seen, we would try to reduce the number of opiates they were taking, offering to substitute with a less addictive or nonaddictive treatment option. With rare exceptions, they would refuse to even consider a change. "You don't know my pain" became the most common line I heard in my clerkship. The patients were truly suffering, many with real physical injuries, but they had come to define themselves by their pain, and they demanded that everyone else accede to this identity. Most of them had lost all meaning in their lives outside of fetishizing their physical pain.

To move past narcissism, you must develop meaning in your life. No one else can do it for you. The development of meaning must follow the development of values, as described above. One follows the other. Without a set of clear values, you will pursue a failed path (or many failed paths) of emotionally driven or circumstantially forced pursuits, like many of the patients I see in my practice. Most Los Angelenos have relocated from other cities and states, fleeing from disappointing circumstances. Rarely have they invested much energy in clarifying what their values are, so when they fling themselves into modeling and acting, they are invariably led in a direction that results in significant psychological injury. They often begin using drugs and engage in transactional sex to work their way toward better roles.

One twenty-seven-year-old arrived at my office for an evaluation for insomnia, proudly announcing she had just relocated from Alabama to Los Angeles and already had earned a substantial sum producing commercial videos to sell clothing. At first, she came across as confident, strong, and optimistic. Over the course of the hour, though, she broke down in tears, confessing that her money had really been earned by dancing topless on Only Fans—an online private peep show. She explained that she had fled an abusive household back home and had hoped to make it big in Los Angeles as an actor. She didn't know who she was, though, and she had become seduced by the attention she was receiving, so much so that she began to cross a boundary that was visible to her only after the fact. The lack of meaning in her life had led her to make decisions that not only prevented her from sleeping but also destroyed any sense of identity she held, redefining her value as nothing more than a girl with a body for sale. You must first define your values and then work on developing meaning in your life by acting in concert with them.

When you remain preoccupied with yourself, you risk becoming a victim to all sorts of mental illnesses:

anxiety disorders, depression, delusional thinking, and addiction. Fear addiction stems from that self-preoccupation. The hyperfocus on your own emotional state precludes real empathy with others, who become nothing more than glorified cheerleaders for the undeveloped baby who lies inside you. Development can occur only when the focus shifts to the outside to others to the accomplishments uniquely available to each person. Pursuing a life of purpose and meaning, guided by well-considered values, is the antidote to narcissistic preoccupation. It is also a potent treatment for fear addiction.

Reject narcissism. Your fear doesn't matter to society—*you* do. The real you.

Step 5

Cut Off the Dealer: Eliminate Media Fear Junkies

A sixty-year-old married woman came to my office on the verge of a nervous breakdown. "After forty years of marriage, I feel like I no longer know my husband," she told me. When I asked her why, she replied, "I've been living a full life for the past two years, continuing to work, seeing friends, traveling...he calls me crazy, full of stupid and dangerous ideas, refusing to keep myself safe." I asked her what he had been doing. "He just sits in front of the TV all day, watching CNN," she said.

Her husband had developed a fear addiction, courtesy of cable news.

Perhaps above all else, the media has driven and sustained a nationwide addiction to fear. It has acted as a drug dealer, luring customers with the promise of exciting information, only to provide sensationalism and lies seasoned with out-of-context alarmist hyperbole. It's captivating to watch and listen to, though, and once the customer is hooked, he keeps coming back for more.

For decades, local television news has been known for attracting viewers at the top of a broadcast hour with the criterion "If it bleeds, it leads." Psychologically, people are attracted to hearing about the misfortunes of others. This probably derives from a sense of relief in thinking, "Thank goodness it isn't me." Paradoxically, this reinforces a sense of safety due to the distance between the viewer and the victim. For the same reason, drivers slow down on the highway when passing an accident. It's more than just an expression of curiosity; people want to reassure themselves that no matter how horrible the accident, *they* remain safe. It didn't happen to *them*. This phenomenon of *schadenfreude* is universal and far from pathologic, but it has been mined for financial gain by reporters for longer than I can remember.

Recently, though, something significant changed. Rather than simply luring viewers with a tantalizing hook to redirect attention, like retail shops employing a few loss leaders to draw customers into the store, the media has chosen to fully stock every shelf with highly addictive junk food, guaranteeing that its customers will become both addicted to the nonnutritious content and psychologically unhealthy. Its previous mission to inform (and, to some degree, entertain) has been entirely replaced by the single-minded pursuit of activating an emotional response to a stimulus more powerful than either love or hate: fear.

This goal of addicting Americans to fear through a screen is not difficult to achieve, particularly with a captured audience. Just as drugs are not appealing to anyone leading a full life whose pleasure comes from the richness of work, relationships, and personal growth, a diet of fear does not attract anyone occupied with deeply meaningful pursuits based on real, lived connections to people, projects, and nature. Since 2020, many Americans have been forced into, or have chosen, a life of physical confinement and social constraint, rendering them vulnerable to the dealer living in their phones, computers, and televisions. When you don't leave your home, the media no longer needs to compete for your attention. You become an easy target.

It is undeniable that the media has made Americans afraid—chronically afraid. If every morning the first thing you read is a death count on page one of the *New York Times*, the push alert on the phone from Yahoo News, or the chyron scrolling across the bottom of the television screen on MSNBC, even if you do happen to leave your home, the seed has been planted. You've been injected with a dose of fear that orients you in the direction of feeling unsafe. And the number of deaths keeps rising every day! Rarely is there ever any context provided, such as the ages and comorbidities of the dead. You conclude that you could be next. Death is everywhere. It's like living in medieval Europe during the plague, except that rather than watching carts pass by on the street, piled high with corpses, all you need to do to feel the depth and extent of the threat is glance at your phone. This is a state of emergency, or so you are told.

Let's rewind to 2020. Perhaps you decide to turn off the daily news and relax on the sofa with a periodical. You pick up the September issue of *The Atlantic*, titled "HOW DID IT COME TO THIS?" to be met with the headline, "Why the Virus Won." That sounds rather bleak. You set that down and instead turn to the September 21st issue of *Time* magazine lying beside it. Entirely black, white, and gray, the cover is littered with random dates, numbers, and the word "deaths" printed in a ghoulish font, as one large number—200,000—appears across the page, superimposed, with three distinct words written in blood red occupying the solid black bottom third: "An American Failure." Definitely not bedtime reading. You glance at the September 20th *NYT* sitting on the breakfast table. The page A1 headline reads, "'We May Be Surprised Again': An Unpredictable Pandemic Takes a Terrible Toll."

What to do? You'd like to just go outside and take a walk, but that requires a mask, and if you see someone approaching from the other direction, the new social decorum dictates that either one of you cross to the other side of the street or jump into oncoming traffic. Of course, you could always simply stand on the curb with your back facing the stranger while you hold your breath until he passes by. Feeling weary from the thought, you decide to simply stay in. If someone rings the doorbell, you don't need to answer the door, because you have a Ring camera and can say, "Just leave whatever it is on the porch. I'll come pick it up after dark." Have to stay safe.

You keep reading interviews describing how other people, mostly women, disinfect their Amazon packages before bringing them indoors. Some of them require their husbands to disrobe in the garage when they come home from work and toss their clothing in the dryer for a full heat cycle before they're allowed in the house. No one in the media finds this the least bit odd. Don Lemon, Joy Reid, and Anderson Cooper all praise these behaviors as worthy of emulation by every American. "Out of an abundance of caution" are the operating words that preface every news report, especially when the newscaster is introducing the latest mandate by the state governor, city mayor, or unelected bureaucrat running the county health department. There is no disagreement. If anything, the news anchors criticize the timing of any given measure as coming a bit too late: "We really should have been doing this sooner...all of us."

At some point, sensationalist news transformed into pure propaganda. *Pravda* provided more truth than all American media combined. I have a friend who likes to proudly remind everyone that he reads and listens to "several news sources" so he can be sure he's being exposed to the full spectrum of viewpoints. What are those sources? "I look at CNN, NBC, the *NYT*, and the *Wall Street Journal*," he says. That's when I remind him that he's exposing himself to only two different views, because the first three are redundant. (And outside of its editorial pages, the *Journal* is, for all intents and purposes, a liberal paper.) My friend believes that if three out of four agree with one another, that must mean their shared opinion is the correct one. I ascribe this to the fallacy of assuming majority rule represents a moral position, as in, "Two wolves and a sheep vote on what to have for dinner."

It's bad enough that what is called "mainstream news" has become nothing more than an echo chamber for one point of view, often containing very little truth and quite a bit of propaganda. Many Americans today, especially the youth, don't follow cable news, don't read newspapers or periodicals, and don't watch talk shows. They obtain nearly 100 percent of their information from social media. Few realize that all these "news sources" rely on algorithms and aggregators to funnel and filter a message that bears no resemblance to actual news. Facebook, Yahoo, Google, LinkedIn, WhatsApp, TikTok, Instagram, Microsoft, and Apple all are owned by China or a small circle of individuals whose interests do not align with those of most

Americans. You could open news push notifications or links all day long from every one of these companies and their software and never encounter an opposing opinion.

Worse, individual messages or posts of other news sources may be restricted from access by an advisory warning, redirect the user to a government website like the CDC or the FDA, or simply be removed entirely, if the content strays from what the corporate owners agree with. When I posted a link on LinkedIn to a documentary titled *Unmask Your Child*, it was taken down in less than a week, with a message that read, "This content places the community at risk of physical harm." Just as WhatsApp and Instagram are owned by Facebook, which is managed by Mark Zuckerberg, LinkedIn is owned by Microsoft, which is run by Bill Gates. Everything on these sites, from private posts to "news" pushes—even Google search results—is curated by employees of the companies that own and manage the software.

In this way, social media should be viewed as a drug dealer whose primary goal is to keep the consumer hooked and coming back for more, as often as possible. Reminding him how dangerous the world, especially his own backyard, has become is the most psychologically powerful way to do it.

A therapy patient of mine in her early twenties had been making excellent progress in overcoming her anxiety about living away from home. Born and raised in Beverly Hills, she had commuted to college while continuing to live with her parents. The environment was not healthy for her emotionally, with a controlling mother and a distant father, but she found it difficult to even consider living on her own. When she finally found the courage to rent a small studio apartment in the downtown Los

Angeles arts district, she experienced real freedom for the first time in her life.

Just as she was about to begin confronting her parents for their emotional neglect, supported by some modest geographical distance, she terminated treatment. "It just isn't safe anymore to come to your office. I keep reading on my phone how dangerous it's become. I really shouldn't even be going outside." I reminded her how much stronger and healthier she had become in only a few months of work, pointing out the independence she had built by finding an apartment for herself and moving away from home. "Yeah...about that...I really think it's better for me to go back home," she said. "We may be on full lockdown soon. I might not even be able to drive anywhere anymore. If that happens, it's better for me to be at home with my parents."

That was the last time I saw her. She did reappear one year later, phoning me to ask if I would see her over Zoom. Clearly, she wanted (and needed) treatment. Fear had overtaken her, though, and her insulation from real information had made it impossible for her to make rational decisions. She couldn't cut off her dealer—her social media—and chose to maintain her addiction at her safe house, under the watchful eyes of her parents.

Two years later, very little has changed. The media's commitment to maintaining its customers' fear addiction is so powerful that even good news is intentionally infused with fright.

The *Los Angeles Daily News*' weekly travel section had all but stopped reporting anything related to cruises, as there had been none for over a year. In 2022, however, the ships began sailing again. Rather than celebrate the return of sea travel, the paper focused on the "wave of infection" striking every ship, in spite of the requirement that every passenger be "fully vaccinated." One particularly egregious example focused on a recent excursion to the Caribbean, soberly detailing the absurd and paranoid protocols passengers were required to follow throughout the cruise. In addition to having mandatory mRNA injections, everyone had to wear a mask at all times while on board (even during comedy shows), get tested every seventy-two hours, and never congregate in groups larger than four people.

A highlight of one article was the exiling of a young, healthy crew member to the "red zone" of the ship after he had received an asymptomatic positive test midway through the trip. Although "alarming," aggressive intervention by the cruise's managers successfully tracked down every passenger the hapless crew member had been near and placed them in the red zone for fourteen-day isolation as well...for the whole ten-day cruise. Even the writer himself acknowledged the clear lack of utility of the safety practices, noting that at every port, cruise passengers were free to leave the ship and explore the town mask-free until their return at the end of the day.

The cruise sounded like a floating concentration camp, but what struck me most was how gleefully the paper reported on the fear-driven measures used to terrorize the passengers and crew. It felt perversely masochistic—the elevation of fear as a noble quality necessary for a successful vacation. This type of journalism has become the norm.

How do you release yourself from the grip of the drug-dealing media? One of my millennial patients swapped his smartphone out for a flip phone. He had become so engrossed with the incessant barrage of incendiary fear announcements that he found himself unable to study, to work, to fall asleep. Increasing doses of benzodiazepines led him down a path of near nonfunctionality, until he decided to cut the dealer off completely and shut the phone down for good. Without the reflexive need to check his phone all day long, he became able to relax and return his focus to his studies and part-time job. His anxiety diminished, and his mood improved. Then he was able to back off the anxiolytic medication and sleep normally again.

I certainly do not suggest that you isolate yourself from the world. My patient abandoned his smartphone but discovered a curiosity for real information, and he began seeking the information himself rather than waiting for it to be delivered to him through his phone. He took charge of his own education.

Most Americans today consume news and information passively, waiting to be fed at regular intervals by their devices. They exercise no control or decision-making over what they are absorbing. Just as a lazy diet of junk food will lead to obesity, the passive consumption of fear porn masquerading as news will provoke a chronic fear state. The first step, then, in combating fear addiction through media is to make your own choices in what you read, watch, and listen to.

Accept that all media is biased. Bias is not the problem—dishonesty is. Often, patients ask me how to go about finding media that is "unbiased." There is no such thing. A better question to ask is, "What source offers the most truth?" That question is difficult to answer at one moment in time. It becomes much easier to discern who is telling the truth, however, by looking backward. What did a given source state one year ago, and did it turn out to be true or a lie?

When evaluated this way, most sources will display a pattern of either telling truths or spreading lies. If an error was made, was it acknowledged as soon as it was discovered? Everyone makes mistakes, but not everyone owns up to them. There is no point in following news that displays a pattern of lying or making frequent "mistakes" that are not acknowledged. You can be certain the writers have an agenda, and it is not to inform their readers.

If you are unable to discern between a drug dealer and a fruit vendor, then you may need to temporarily avoid making any street purchases. Perhaps your addiction to fear has become so strong that you have lost your capacity to objectively evaluate the product being sold. Placing a temporary hold on all media consumption will not lead to starvation.

Think of it as a fast, or perhaps a cleanse. A recalibration is in order. Shut off all the screens and power down the devices. Leave the newspapers and periodicals alone. Pick up a novel and become reacquainted with yourself and your inner world. You probably no longer know what it is to feel genuine self-generated emotion. Your entire psychological state has been driven and maintained by outside forces, all intent on capturing you emotionally and compelling you to return again and again for more "education," as you gradually lose all agency.

That is the goal of the dealer. He tells you he is giving you what you need, but he is doing nothing of the sort. He is depriving you of your capacity to think critically by paralyzing you with fear.

Imagine that you have just decided to give up drinking. You walk home from work every day with the option of passing by an open bar during happy hour. You will see patrons enjoying an early drink on the patio, laughing and talking. You will be able to smell the alcohol. How many times will you be able to walk past the bar without stepping inside? Your other option is to walk down a different street lined with bookstores and coffee shops. If you choose this path, your attention will be drawn to reading and espresso rather than beer and wine. Your odds of maintaining sobriety will have increased dramatically.

A similar example can be found in what foods you decide to purchase. If you are trying to lose weight, stocking your kitchen with healthy snacks will ensure that when you become hungry, you will not be eating chips and ice cream but rather fruits and vegetables. You could always leave your home, drive to the store, and buy a chocolate cake, but that would require effort. It's much easier to satisfy your cravings with what you keep in front of you.

For that reason, eliminating the option of consuming unhealthy media by removing it from your environment can be a powerful source of protection from fear addiction. Shut off all the push notifications from your phone—from Apple News+, Facebook, and any other application that makes its own decision when and what to send to you. If you want to participate in social media for purely social reasons, pick a time of day and a duration of time—twenty minutes, for example—when you'll read and respond to posts from friends. Outside of that window, keep the software muted or simply log out of it entirely. When you wake up in the morning or come home from work, keep the TV turned off. Listen to music instead, or an audiobook you've been interested in reading. Exercise some control and discipline over what you consume. You will be amazed at how freeing it is to know that you are the one making the decisions.

Focus on exposing yourself to words, images, and sounds that instill courage rather than fear. More than any art form, music has the power to bypass the intellect and transfer an emotional experience. Seek out music that you find inspiring and energizing. Read about men and women who faced danger with strength and conviction, who overcame fear to accomplish great things. Choose films that show people taking risks and conquering adversity. Although you will not find them represented in entertainment today, heroes abound in older films and literature. They are not hard to locate, if you make the effort to look for them. You become what you consume, whether it's food or an emotional experience.

If you share the company of fearless, life-affirming, risk-taking individuals—real or fictional—their stories will rub off on you. Your inner world will become filled with adventure and accomplishment, and you will begin to express it outwardly through the actions you take in your own life.

There may come a time when you have developed enough resilience to be able to tolerate some exposure to lying, fearmongering media. When you come across it, you'll see through the false presentation of "news" for what it really is—indoctrination, propaganda, and a sinister attempt to hook you into not looking away. It will feel distasteful and nauseating. You will recognize the poison right away. This process can unfold, however, only if you choose to distance yourself from the legacy media. And it *is* a choice. No one can do it for you.

Cut off the dealer. Eliminate the media and invite the fearless into your life.

Step 6

Think for Yourself: Or Others Will Think for You

When I began speaking publicly in spring 2020, I was often asked, "What is the one thing that we can all do to fight back against the mass delusional psychosis?" My answer: "Think for yourself." I emphasized this point in my first book, *United States of Fear*, where I explained the causes of the mass delusional psychosis that had overtaken the nation in 2020. One of those causes was the near total abdication, on the part of most Americans, of independent thought. By granting others the power to think on their behalf, the majority of the population has allowed themselves to be deceived by massive lies propagated by the government, the media, and large corporations. It's time to take that responsibility back.

My goal, in both my clinical practice and my talks throughout the country, has never been to tell people *what* to think. What I attempt to do is encourage Americans to think critically, use their own minds, and always question what they are being told. I advise everyone I speak with to go beyond Ronald Reagan's teaching "Trust but verify."

Today the approach must be "Trust nothing and no one until verified."

As I explained in the previous chapter, the degree and breadth of omission, misinformation, and outright lying throughout the media over the past several years rivals that of twentieth-century dictatorships like the Soviet Union. When it comes to overcoming fear addiction, training yourself to think independently by exercising your mind is a daily practice that you must start immediately. Without independent thought, there is no way out of fear addiction. Freedom from fear requires freedom from external control.

New Zealand's prime minister, Jacinda Ardern, announced in a news conference in July 2021, "Unless you hear it from us, it is not the truth." As Ardern is the leader of a country that is best known for its sheep, perhaps it should not be surprising to hear her say, "We will continue to be your single source of truth." Unfailingly, what the residents of New Zealand have heard for over two years has been nothing other than "Be afraid. Be very afraid." They have been ordered to remain in their homes, not go to work, and allow dying relatives in the hospital to spend their final days alone.

Why? Because normal living is too dangerous. Anyone who says otherwise is, according to the prime minister, lying. Sadly, most of the residents there have allowed people like Ardern, who is certainly not thinking of them, to make decisions on behalf of themselves and their children.

We have seen the same thing here in the United States. Federal government agencies such as the Centers for Disease Control and the Food and Drug Administration have been lying to the American people from the beginning of the pandemic. From attacking the safety and efficacy of proven treatments for viral infection to promoting masks as a reliable form of protection, what many people have long considered to be trusted sources of information and advice have proven themselves to be thoroughly corrupt and beholden to political and financial interests.

Anthony Fauci, the de facto unelected president of the United States since 2020, has been exposed as a liar so frequently by U.S. senator Rand Paul (Republican from Kentucky) in their very public confrontations during congressional hearings that it is astonishing anyone continues to believe a word he says. And yet many Americans still regard him as their single source of truth, just as New Zealanders are ordered to view their own Ministry of Health as such.

Dishonest government advisers certainly should be held responsible for failing their constituents, but the people who take their advice at face value, without challenge or thoughtful critique, must acknowledge their role as well in the development of their fear addiction—"Fool me twice, shame on me." How many hundreds of times have you allowed yourself to be fooled over the past three years simply because you failed to think critically about what you were told?

It is certainly understandable that some Americans were caught flat-footed in March 2020, did not know what to do about the threat of a deadly virus spreading throughout the country, and panicked. They assumed their government had their best interests at heart, so they went along with the extreme measures initially announced. After the first two weeks, however, information readily available to the public showed that there was little reason for 98 percent of the population to be afraid. The fear persisted and expanded, in spite of this, accelerating the spread of fear addiction in those who chose not to think independently but to rely on government pronouncements and guidelines grounded in politics rather than science. That is not Anthony Fauci's fault—it is their own. By not questioning directives that defy all common sense, many Americans have allowed themselves to be dragged into a turbulent river of fear, eventually ceding all means to navigate their own lives.

I began pointing out the decline in critical thinking skills long before the arrival of the Wuhan virus in 2020. I often quote Thoreau, who said, "Think for yourself, or others will think for you without thinking of you." I emphasize this point frequently with my patients, who suffer from emotional pain because they grant power to other people to think on their behalf. Each person is responsible not only for his own happiness but also for his own thoughts. He is responsible for putting forth the effort required to be an active, rather than passive, participant in the events of life that affect him. This can be done only by thinking critically.

As much as education in this country has removed critical thinking from the curriculum over the past decade, the source of the problem is not only a lack of formal training. I have met many older Americans educated at a time when propaganda was not the primary tool wielded in the schools, and the phrase "diversity, equity, and inclusion" was not the mission statement (or manifesto) in nearly every American corporation. Even these older Americans display little to no interest in critically evaluating what they are being told by their government representatives. Just as they eagerly await their Social Security checks from Washington every month, they dutifully follow federal pronouncements to cancel their upcoming in-person medical appointments "until it's safe" to attend them.

Sadly, this foolish advice has led to the early deaths of countless older Americans who failed to monitor their blood pressure or blood sugar, obtain cancer screenings, or seek medical help for cardiac pain. Because they stopped thinking for themselves, they cut short their own lives. Their acquiescence to fear accelerated their deaths.

Do not listen to the "experts." There is good reason for the president of the United States, a civilian, to be commander in chief of the armed forces rather than a general. Military leaders advise the president, but decisions are made by someone whom the people elected to represent them—not a career military officer. Experts know the information or data that is important to their field of specialization, but they are not necessarily adept at advising others about how to lead their lives. The focus is intentionally narrow. They often fail to place their knowledge into a broader context. They certainly have no experience in setting priorities or instructing an individual on how he should weigh risks and benefits in his own life. In the best-case scenario, they can provide current and accurate data that one can use to make one's own decisions.

Physicians are often some of the worst givers of advice. Specialists, in particular, see the world through such a highly filtered and distorted lens that they can rarely apply their knowledge to the broader population. I trained under an anesthesiologist in medical school who spent most of her time responding to "codes," which is hospital speak for when a patient's heart has stopped or the patient has stopped breathing. Frequently, the cause was a blocked airway. She became adept at performing emergency tracheotomies, surgical procedures that create an opening in the throat to allow a person to breathe when the nose or mouth is obstructed.

Once during a teaching session, she reached for her purse and removed a credit card with a sharpened edge. "I carry this old credit card that I've cut at an angle with a pair of scissors, so that if I'm on a plane without any metal tools (prohibited by the Transportation Security Administration), I'll be able to create an airway if one of the passengers stops breathing." She then recommended that we all carry one as well.

I have flown multiple times a year for decades and have never seen a passenger on a plane stop breathing due to an airway obstruction that could not be cleared using the Heimlich maneuver. This type of emergency is extremely rare—as rare as a healthy person dying of influenza or the coronavirus—yet she saw it all the time in the hospital, due to the nature of her work. In her eyes, every healthy American is a walking potential airway obstruction. That is how she views the world—and how she advised us to view it.

My recent conversations with colleagues who work in tertiary care hospitals—where the sickest patients are sent—reflect the same expert bias. I have tried to explain to them that for the average American, worrying about dying from the Wuhan virus is about as useful or rational as worrying about dying from a car accident. Their response is to point out how they see patients dying in the intensive care unit every day, as if to prove that death is a common outcome of a highly contagious but largely innocuous respiratory viral infection. One internist even told me, "I don't want to see patients in the hospital anymore, because I don't want to bring this back to my family."

This man has treated hospitalized patients for more than thirty years—patients with HIV and AIDS, tuberculosis, hepatitis, MRSA. Not once has he ever, to my knowledge, said anything like that before. Now he is spreading his own fear to patients and staff in his private practice, urging everyone to get experimental mRNA injections, wear masks, stay home, not go to school, and so on. His staff and patients trust him because he is the expert, yet his advice makes no sense for most, if not all, of the people he offers it to.

The only way anyone can protect himself from developing an addiction to the fearmongering of his personal physician is to think independently, ask questions, and reach a decision that makes sense for his situation. Had more Americans done this, they would not have developed the chronic fear state that they continue to suffer from today.

I'm often called to participate in depositions for medical-legal cases, for which I provide my clinical opinions to the court. Throughout the pandemic, I insisted that all depositions be conducted in person, as this provides the best transcript. Anything done through Zoom or Skype is vulnerable to internet connectivity issues, as well as two or more parties frequently talking over one another. Most attorneys understand this and feel the same way, so they have largely been agreeable to continuing with in-person depositions, even if they insist on showing up wearing a mask.

As late as early 2022, however, one attorney insisted she would not consider an in-person deposition with me under any condition due to "the new variant." She hadn't asked herself the most basic question, "Is my risk from catching the new variant any greater than my risk from catching a common cold?" This woman continues to eat in restaurants seated with other people, fully exposed to the air around her (and without a mask, while seated). She continues to fly on airplanes, breathing the same air as the person twelve inches away for hours at a time. For her, this all makes perfect sense, because she compliantly follows orders given by her local health department bureaucrats.

As an attorney, she is required to exercise critical thinking when working on behalf of her clients. Sadly, she has chosen not to think critically at all when it comes to her own health. In this domain, she has allowed others to think for her.

Delegation of individual decision-making has become a major problem in our society. We pay for home meal delivery services to decide what we will eat for dinner, and we allow Netflix to decide what series or movie we watch after one ends. "Suggestions" from Facebook, Apple, Twitter, and Instagram flood our cell phones, redirecting our attention to sites, feeds, posts, and products that benefit primarily the producers of that information. Deciding takes time and energy, so many people are only too happy to hand that responsibility over to others.

Falling out of practice with making little decisions, though, can lead to delegating more important decision-making. How many parents have bought into the lie that their children benefit from the Wuhan virus "vaccine"? What starts out as grocery shopping avoidance grows into an abdication of your parental autonomy and responsibility for deciding what drugs are injected into your child's body.

Weak men often display this in their relationships with women. When a wife asks, "Where are we going to eat tonight?" a weak man will reply, "Wherever you want is fine with me." This man has relinquished his agency to decide for himself and his wife. He has chosen to *not* be a leader. He is training himself to be a sheep—someone who waits for direction from the shepherd. In this case, he is asking his wife to guide him.

From whom will he receive his guidance when it comes to his physical health and safety? Anthony Fauci? The prime minister of New Zealand? If he is told that he should feel afraid and act accordingly, why would he question that guidance, much less object to it, when he doesn't even accept the burden of choosing a restaurant for himself and his wife? The total abdication of individual autonomy begins with small, seemingly insignificant acts of delegation.

What should you do to break this insidious habit? Assert yourself. You are the expert when it comes to *you*. Human beings have not evolved to be herds of sheep. We can and should think for ourselves; we should question and challenge what we are being told every day. When you hear that due to an emergency, you are no longer entitled to make your own decisions and that those you have elected to represent you no longer have the right to advocate on your behalf—that only unaccountable "experts" are now able to decide whether you work, study, or leave your home—that should sound an alarm. It should provoke suspicion and scrutiny. It should energize you to demand clear and convincing evidence that ceding your core freedoms is both justified and in your best interests. And you should continue to press that demand frequently, for as long as you are asked to defer to the "experts." If you do not, your entire life may be stripped from you, as you remain paralyzed with fear and unable to take action, because you are no longer thinking for yourself.

In Hans Christian Andersen's famous story of the naked emperor, no adult dares to challenge what he has been told by the "expert" tailors. All the adults are motivated by fear to join the herd praising the beauty of the invisible garments on display. Although they know better, their fear of being judged and called stupid for exposing the truth robs them of their ability to think clearly. They defer to the corrupt, lying conmen pretending to be artisanal weavers. Eventually, the truth is exposed—by a child—and the weakness of the adults is revealed for all to see.

For us, it is never too late to acknowledge that we have been fooled. Thinking for oneself often requires admitting to having been made a fool of. There is no shame in that. The real shame comes from maintaining a chronic state of fear that all but guarantees weakness. The fear addict is always weak because choosing to think independently would lead to strength and the banishment of fear. Fear addiction is a passive condition. Passivity is reactive. The locus of control lies outside oneself.

Retake control of your life and move beyond your fear addiction by thinking for yourself. Do not allow others to think for you.

Step 7

Accountability: Acknowledge the Harm Your Fear Has Caused Yourself and Others

In 1994, Hutu tribesmen in Rwanda massacred one million Tutsis, often dismembering their victims with machetes. The genocide was so widespread, involving a majority of the population from both tribes, that many doubted the country could recover from it. This doubt stemmed not just from the sheer number of dead and maimed Rwandans. Every surviving Tutsi knew someone who had died, as well as a Hutu responsible for murder. How would it be possible for anyone to continue to live next door to the murderer of his brother, sister, or father? And what if the entire nation were left in this unimaginable position? The situation appeared to be impossible.

The impossible was resolved, however, through a process called truth and reconciliation. Although an international criminal tribunal and a national court system tried and convicted the worst offenders, the Rwandans knew that it would not be possible to conduct hundreds of thousands of trials of members of the general population. So they agreed to set aside the most severe criminal penalties for those responsible in exchange for a public acknowledgment of wrongdoing offered to the victims or the victims' survivors.

A local commission was set up in every village so that the victims, their families, and others could witness the perpetrators publicly account for their crimes. Every injury and every murder would be documented. Most of the attacks were not random—the murderers knew their victims. Although this solution was far from perfect, it was the best one the Rwandan people could devise, and it did succeed in bringing the country back together. By acknowledging the harm their reign of terror had brought, the Hutu population saved itself from social ostracism or permanent banishment.

The death count in the United States from the Wuhan virus rivals that of the Rwandan genocide. One million Americans reportedly died of the virus between 2020 and 2022. Although already clearly exaggerated, as the CDC itself has acknowledged that at least 94 percent of those deaths occurred in people with multiple serious comorbidities, the actual number of deaths would have been reduced even further by at least several hundred thousand, perhaps more, had the sick been offered early treatment. Those individuals who intentionally blocked treatment—the politicians, unelected bureaucrats, and corporate executives of hospitals and pharmacies—should be tried in criminal court and imprisoned, if found guilty. They are murderers.

Millions of Americans inadvertently caused harm to themselves and others, though, due to fear addiction. They did not set out to kill. They paralyzed themselves and their capacity to make sound decisions because they allowed their fear to control them. Their fear addiction led to significant damage to their emotional and physical health. In many cases, it also led to injury to their family members, friends, and local communities. This harm must be acknowledged, both to regain others' trust and to overcome the addiction.

A seventy-two-year-old widow withdrew from the world in mid-2020, isolating herself at home and going out only to purchase critical supplies such as food, toilet paper, and medicine. She previously had been fit, but her new sedentary life led to significant weight gain. She became depressed. Her fear addiction spiraled out of control until the deterioration of both her mind and body transformed her into a different person entirely.

One day in summer 2021, she woke up, looked in the mirror, and thought, "I don't like the person I've become. This is not the life I want." She left her home (maskless), drove to a local store, and began speaking to anyone she ran into. After a full year of living alone, she had become hungry for the company and conversation of others. She began exercising again. She noticed men noticing her, and she announced, "I want to be in a relationship again." She began to date. As her weight declined, her mood lifted. When I last saw her, I asked what had allowed her to break free of her fear addiction. She replied, "I realized one day that I wasn't keeping myself safe—I was hurting myself. And there was no reason for it. How many years do I have left? I will not be spending them hiding at home alone in fear."

This woman overcame her fear by recognizing the harm it was causing her. Once she did that, it was impossible for her to continue to lie to herself and pretend that her addiction was keeping her alive. On the contrary, it was killing her. And she wanted to live.

Obesity, drinking, social isolation, educational delays, anxiety, depression, loss of creativity and growth—these are all examples of the harm that fear addiction brings. Because addiction is always maintained by lies, the fear addict may be in denial that any of these conditions are present or that it is his uncontrolled fear that has given rise to them.

If addiction caused no harm, there would be little argument against it. Having an addiction would be like having just another hobby. I don't particularly enjoy golf, but I rarely judge others who enjoy playing it. I do judge addiction because it is self-injurious. My pointing out the harm it causes the patient, however, is not very helpful unless he can accept the truth of what I am saying.

I know that an addict is ready to move forward in treatment when I hear him acknowledge how his addiction has hurt him and continues to hurt him. In essence, the power of this acknowledgment lies in its humble acceptance of truth and reality. It represents an internal shift away from omnipotence and toward the conscious realization that one's power, knowledge, and life are finite.

This is always painful to some degree, yet it is necessary for growth. No one can do this for the addict. The change must come from within. He must see with his own eyes how debilitated he has become, how he has fallen short of his potential, and how he has cheated himself by pretending that there is no price to be paid for pursuing his addiction to the exclusion of all else.

I hear so many people continue to blame the Wuhan virus for their anxiety and depression, when it's their own unchallenged addiction to fear that is causing their mental illness. It would be equally foolish for an alcoholic to blame cold winters for his alcoholism, thinking, "I always need to warm up at night, and the whiskey protects me from the cold." Of course, were he to move to Florida, he would use the opposite excuse to rationalize his habit of drinking frozen margaritas after work every weeknight, thinking, "They help me beat the heat."

I have a high school–age patient who had been suffering from mild symptoms of an obsessive-compulsive disorder for many years, with his focus being contagious disease. He was fully aware of his disorder and would readily admit to the harm it was causing him, whenever the symptoms would temporarily worsen. He lost this awareness, though, when he developed a fear addiction in 2020—fear of infection from the Wuhan virus. He wouldn't go to school, wouldn't leave his home, and wouldn't come to my office for his regular visits. The only way I could communicate with him was through Zoom or Skype. He developed insomnia, gained weight, and lost friends.

When I pointed out how his physical and psychological health had declined, he denied that he was suffering. His father became concerned but felt impotent in confronting the addiction. This patient had allowed his fear addiction to take over and hobble his ability to take ownership of the self-harm he was engaging in. Unfortunately, within his peer group, similar behavior had become the norm, so there was little external pressure placed on him to stimulate more accountability. I fear that until he looks in the mirror one day, as my elderly female patient did, and reels from the shock of what he sees, his addiction will continue to spiral out of control, leading to more physical and psychological harm.

Fear addiction doesn't lead only to self-harm; it also leads to societal harm. Acknowledging the harm to oneself first, though, is a prerequisite for taking stock of the harm it causes others. Without self-awareness and accountability, it is difficult to face the external environment with honesty and conviction. Owning up to the damage done to friends, family, and strangers is a more public act than acknowledging how one has hurt oneself. Moreover, one may not be offered forgiveness even when one shows contrition. When someone has hurt others, he is obliged to apologize, but he is not entitled to having his apology accepted.

Facing anger, resentment, judgment, and rejection from those you have wronged requires emotional resilience and maturity. It is humbling to place yourself in a position of vulnerability, not knowing how the other person will respond. Ceding control, though, is nothing new. You accepted that outcome when you chose to pursue an addiction to fear. Now you must recognize that part of the process of freeing yourself from your addiction is placing yourself in a potential line of fire from those you have victimized—whether you intended to hurt them or not.

Don't forget that your lack of intent to harm does nothing to absolve you of the obligation to make amends. The greatest harm to others, and to society as a whole, comes from the utterly misguided intentions of good people. Your otherwise good character does not negate the havoc your fear addiction has wrought on everyone around you.

Although you felt virtuous at the time, your fear addiction may have led you to terrorize your fellow citizens on the street and in stores. If you acted like a "Karen," chasing after strangers and ordering them to put their masks on or measure out six feet of space around them, it's time to own up and speak to your community. Go to the website Nextdoor and post an apology to your local community. Make it specific. For example: "I was unable to manage my fear addiction, and I accosted my fellow shoppers at Ralphs every Tuesday for eighteen months. I publicly mask-shamed them, and I encouraged security to have them thrown out of the store. I was wrong to do that. I know that I hurt many of you. And I'm sorry."

If you victimized your neighbors while taking your daily walk, go knock on their doors and issue a similar apology. They may no longer want to have anything to do with you, so perhaps they won't answer. In that case, leave them a written note. Going about your life pretending none of this happened would be a grave error. Do not rob yourself of the opportunity to make amends, whether it be to those you know by name or to strangers.

I know of many marriages that may not survive because of unresolved fear addiction in one of the spouses. I recently counseled a couple that was contemplating a divorce. They have one child, whom the mother courageously fought to protect from the abusive mandates—masks, antisocial distancing, injections. Her husband suffers from fear addiction, though, and blocked her efforts whenever he could. He told other parents that his wife was not "following the guidelines," going so far as to call child protective services when she allowed their son to play with other children.

To his credit, during our session, he acknowledged that he had been wrong and apologized to his wife. "I made a mistake," he said. "I was only doing what I thought was right, but I screwed up, and I hurt both of you. I'm sorry." I don't know if their marriage will survive, but the tension between them noticeably subsided by the end of the hour. They decided to return and continue the work in a second session.

Many caring, rational Americans have been forced to sever ties with their fear-addicted friends. Trust has been broken. Understandably, to protect themselves from further injury, they have placed friendships on hold. If you are aware of having harmed your friends through your fear addiction, pick up the phone and let them know that you regret having allowed your illness to hurt them. Your goal should not be to repair the relationship, although that may well occur, but simply to make amends.

One of my teenage patients came to realize that his frequent attacks on his friends for continuing to live their lives without fear were not righteous or just, but rather an act of cruelty born of his own fear addiction. He admitted as much to each friend he had mistreated, and he was fortunate to receive their forgiveness. It will take time to rebuild the broken trust, but he has taken the first step.

Acknowledging injuring others may be particularly difficult, and painful, for a parent who has harmed a child. Thousands of American children have already developed myocarditis—a permanent and often crippling cardiac injury—from mRNA injections. Both mothers and fathers have allowed their addiction to fear to lead to what can only be described as child abuse—chronic masking, forced isolation, and the injection of harmful drugs with the stated intent of "keeping them safe."

Of course, the first step is to cease these injurious practices immediately. Next is to explain to your children that while you believed you were protecting them, you were acting purely out of fear. Your fear led you to be irresponsible and fail in your duties as a parent. You harmed them. You cannot equivocate on this by saying something like, "I didn't know any better. Everyone else was doing it. It seemed necessary at the time."

These are all excuses employed by the addict to lessen the sting of responsibility. They are not the words of an individual who truly wishes to be accountable for his actions. It will not be a comfortable or pleasant conversation, but the truth needs to be told. Telling it now will decrease the likelihood that your children will develop resentment toward you as they grow older when they learn that you acted selfishly out of fear rather than following a mature, considered, and deliberate process to truly protect them. You must let them know, though, or you will continue to live with the lie that your fear did not get in the way of your being a good parent in a crisis.

Perhaps the saddest examples of the damage caused by fear addiction are those of adults who refused to see their parents, or who prevented their parents from seeing their grandchildren, during their final years of life. This is an exceptional form of cruelty, as there is little to no time available for the victims to heal. I know grandparents who have not seen their grandchildren in over two years. I know nursing home patients who died alone because their own children refused to visit them.

One man kept himself and his children away from his father for over a year, believing he was protecting him. Only after his father had received an experimental mRNA injection did he allow the family to reunite. Within a few months, his father died of a heart attack. This man deprived his father of his greatest joy—spending time with his family—during his father's final year of life because he could not control his fear addiction. Now he can make amends only through prayer.

Do not allow yourself to suffer needlessly by deferring your own apologies to those you have harmed. Today's opportunity may not be here tomorrow. The time is now. Sweeping your past under the rug may be attractive because it avoids the risk of confrontation and rejection. It also prevents you from moving forward in your life, and it leaves those you have injured without the opportunity to receive the apology they are owed. Surrendering to fear addiction was the easy path that led you to where you are today. Making a purchase on a credit card is easy. Paying it back is not.

It's time to start down the hard road of repairing the damage you have caused, first by acknowledging the damage you have caused to yourself and then by extending your gaze outward to include everyone in your life touched by your fear addiction. This step, perhaps the most difficult, cannot be overlooked or bypassed. Leaving fear behind you does not mean you can leave others—including yourself—behind.

Take accountability. Acknowledge the harm your fear addiction has caused you and others.

Step 8

Embrace Adulthood: Find a Proper Way to Care for Those You Love

One of my adult patients, a woman in her early thirties, doesn't drive. She had always come to her sessions accompanied by her mother, a local university professor. In 2020, her mother became a fear addict and refused to bring my patient to my office. The woman began showing up with her father or dropped off by an Uber driver.

"My mother won't leave the house," she told me. "She's teaching all of her classes remotely. My father and I are doing all the shopping now. She won't touch any of the food we buy until it's been sprayed with a sterilizer. It feels like we're now taking care of her." Her mother had always been somewhat neurotic and anxious, but she had functioned at a high level. Once she allowed her fear to take over, though, she became unable to care for her family. She regressed to the state of a frightened child. Her own daughter had been forced to assume the role of parent.

One of the greatest casualties of addiction is normal development. While you are addicted, you remain in a state of developmental arrest. That means you cannot grow, mature, or deepen your relationships with others. In many cases, such as that of my patient's mother, you actually move backward into a state of primitive tribalism, organized around the addiction itself. Fear becomes your chieftain, to whom you swear all allegiance. This is universal and true for every addiction. You can neither grow into adulthood nor live as an adult while in a state of addiction.

To be clear: Taking care of others does not mean controlling them. A sinister cartoon illustration appeared in late 2020 that showed a masked woman speaking to an unmasked woman. The masked woman said, "Dear, my mask protects you." That lie became the rationale to control an entire population with forced masking and for individuals to coerce others to get on board with the control under the guise of "keeping others safe." This is a perversion of true caretaking rather than a healthy expression of it. It is decidedly not what healthy adults do.

As American teenagers remain at their parents' home longer, often staying years after graduating from college, it has become less clear at what age adulthood begins. When do you become an adult? Is it at age eighteen? Age twenty-two? Age thirty? The answer is rather simple: when you decide to.

We used to rely on rituals to determine when adulthood began. For Jews, it was a Bar or Bat Mitzvah. For Catholics, Confirmation. For Latinos, a quinceañera. For secular Americans, the all-inclusive event of going away to college or enlisting in the military performed a similar but nonreligious function. It would be difficult for anyone to argue today, however, that any of these milestones necessarily leads to maturation or the assuming of adult responsibility. All religious rituals have become purely ceremonial, similar to the role played by British royalty—beloved yet inconsequential in the affairs of day-to-day life. Marriage (and even having a child) means little now. Contemporary college life in America has become nothing more than a four-year stint at a country club, where all personal responsibility is banished in place of universal infantilization.

It appears that the religious or social conventions we used to rely on as markers of a transition into adulthood no longer credibly represent passage into adult society. Even military service no longer provides the necessary reality check that thrusts enlistees into the deep end of life. When expanding diversity, equity, and inclusion replaces fighting for God and country as the American military's manifesto, what hope is there for young Americans to grow and mature as soldiers?

Today, you become an adult the day you choose to. I have patients in their sixties who have yet to make that choice. They continue to live as children, beholden to others to make decisions for them or dependent on the state to pay their living expenses. They blame everyone but themselves for their problems and lack of fulfillment, while they pursue—moment to moment—gratification of their emotional needs, guaranteeing a lack of achievement and meaning in their lives. On the other end of the spectrum, I see teenagers barely out of high school who exhibit such determination to assume adult responsibilities that I feel moved to advise them to slow down and give themselves a bit more time to appreciate what should be a relatively short period, when being fully taken care of is a healthy stage of development. I wish I saw more of this type of patient.

Choosing to become an adult has unfortunately become a struggle for many young Americans. I do have sympathy for them. They are neither encouraged to make the leap nor shown much reason to. Why would you choose to move out of your parents' home, where your every need is taken care of, to assume the role of a generic employee for a soulless company, the majority of your income confiscated in taxes or disappearing every month in rent, as you hold out no hope of ever attaining the financial status of your mother and father, or even of buying a home for yourself? Husbands and fathers are portrayed as fools on television. Soldiers are decried by the media as colonialists. Anyone who attends church or reads the Bible is considered by all good urbanites to be an antiscience, uneducated Luddite who really shouldn't even be voting. As seen in creations such as the "Pajama Boy" meme and the "Life of Julia" story on Barack Obama's website, depicting the embodiment of the emasculated American man and the government-dependent American woman, and Joe Biden's "Life of Linda" presentation (showing a working single mother married to the government), remaining a child and eschewing adulthood for the entirety of one's life has now become the official goal of every American, according to the U.S. government.

By transferring the responsibility to care for yourself, your spouse (if you have one), your children, and your friends onto someone or something else, you deprive yourself of the opportunity to live as an adult. You remain as a child, agreeing to follow the rules in exchange for the promise of being taken care of. A similarly unhealthy process of developmental arrest occurs when you choose to live in a chronic state of fear.

The instinctual curse of wanting to be taken care of above all else is a plague on our society. Yet it must be overcome by any individual who desires to embrace adulthood. Being responsible for yourself and others requires deferring immediate gratification, not acting out of emotion, and tolerating temporary discomfort. And it requires making a choice.

What does embracing adulthood look like? And what is the proper way to care for others? The latter means putting their needs first, rather than your own. It means not projecting your needs onto them. "My mask protects you" is not an expression of caring for others. It is a perversion. George Bernard Shaw wrote, "Do not do unto others as you would that they should do unto you. Their tastes may not be the same."

Ordering your parents or children to wear masks, get injections, and take invasive tests when they're not showing symptoms of illness is not an act of love or caretaking. It is an expression of fear and the desire to control. It is a symptom of fear addiction. It is something to be fought, not modeled. It also can be an expression of a poor ability to manage anger. For a fearful person, witnessing others living freely and without fear can provoke resentment and rage. Whether or not he holds a sincere belief that others are endangering him and acting selfishly, simply witnessing someone thinking for himself becomes a narcissistic injury for the fear addict. The fearful envy the fearless, and envy spoils—as in, "He doesn't deserve to own such a nice car, so I keyed it." In a sick way, society now condones assaults on others and even encourages them—all under the banner of health and safety.

Acknowledging that your fears and anxieties have driven you *away* from properly caring for others removes one of the first obstacles to placing others' needs ahead of your own. When I challenged the adults in Orange County, California, in May 2020 to display proper care for children by reopening the schools there, I mistakenly assumed that I was speaking to a group of adults. I was not. I was speaking to a group largely composed of cowering children, projecting their fear onto their own children, whom they chose to sacrifice on behalf of their fear addiction. What I should have said was, "It's time to grow up. Be adults. Put your children's needs first. Work on your emotional needs on your own time." I underestimated the degree of regression that fear addiction could provoke.

Many adults addicted to fear confuse their emotionally driven frenzy to control others with mature acts of caretaking. They even attack those who rebuff their efforts, questioning their character and threatening them with physical, social, and legal violence. Numerous people have filed formal complaints against me with the Medical Board of California because I have advocated for a universal ban on masking children. They remind me of pseudo adults who refuse to be around children or allow children into their home, because "children break things and spread disease." Yes, they do, especially when there are no real adults around who can set aside their own narcissism and unchecked fear to properly tend to them. Oscar Wilde said, "Selfishness is not living as one wishes to live. It is asking others to live as one wishes to live. And unselfishness is letting other people's lives alone, not interfering with them." The moment one understands this, one makes a significant step toward embracing adulthood.

Choosing to live as an adult also means cutting the ties of dependency on fear to guarantee safety and security. Relying on a drug to take away pain produces a fleeting state of comfort or even pleasure, yet it blocks growth by denying access to reality. Fear addiction does the same. Relying on fear to feel safe constrains you both from properly caring for yourself and from embodying the role of caretaker for others. It impedes risk-taking, shuts you down, and severs your ties with the outside world.

One of my adult patients is autistic. Years ago, he was diagnosed with Asperger syndrome. He has always struggled with making his way in the world due to his limited social skills and poor display of empathy. After falling prey to fear addiction, though, he has regressed and can no longer even keep himself healthy, much less care for others. His obsession with covering his face and physically distancing himself from other human beings precludes any possibility of empathizing with the experiences of his friends and family. Although he is now in his thirties, he behaves like a petulant child, obsessed with his own emotional experience of fear. Previously awkward, he now appears rigid, judgmental, impatient, and highly irritable. I am certain he will remain unable to grow and mature until he chooses to release himself from his fear addiction and starts acting like an adult again.

Choosing to be an adult also means choosing to solve your own problems rather than relying on others to fix them. A young millennial working as a receptionist in a medical office I used to visit was having trouble with the coffee machine one morning. Apparently, there were no more K-cups available for the Keurig machine. Desperate for her morning shot of caffeine, she attempted to use the traditional drip coffee machine, fumbled with the filter, and spilled coffee grounds all over the floor. When the office manager arrived, this young woman was in tears. "I've never had to use this machine before, and I don't know how," she lamented. "We're all out of K-cups."

To reinforce the seriousness of the situation, she then turned to the mess on the floor, pointed at it, and declared, "This—this is a travesty." Not only did she refuse to clean up the mess she had made, but she demanded that the office manager send another employee to the local 7-Eleven for an emergency K-cup run. She was a child in a woman's body, unwilling to accept even the most rudimentary adult responsibilities.

You must embrace discomfort in order to embrace adulthood. There is no such thing as "social distancing." Avoiding people is antisocial, even if it makes you feel "safe." Eliminate distance. Stand close to people. Hug those you know as well as strangers. When you greet someone, offer your hand, not hand sanitizer. When you leave the house, show your face, not your face diaper. Do all of these things because they are what others need, regardless of whether you feel comfortable. In time, it will become second nature, as you develop a habit of acting in an adult capacity that places the needs of others first, rather than feeding your fear addiction through an immature display of childish avoidance. The pursuit of comfort is not an adult occupation.

If you choose to be an adult friend, set aside your fears for a moment and inquire about what the given friend needs from you. The simple question "What can I do to help?" is an adult question, because it acknowledges that the person you are with has needs and that you desire to meet them by subjugating yourself to some degree. The fear addict sees his friends only as sources of support for himself. The proper way to care for a friend is to be of service. That means not using your friend to affirm and then amplify your fears. As you shift your focus away from yourself and toward your friends, you may be surprised to find that the importance you have been placing on your fears diminishes.

If you are a parent and wish to fully embrace the adult role, turn off the TV and sit down with your children. Play a game with them or read them a book. Do not endeavor to be their friend. If your children are older, don't invite them to smoke with you. Establish discipline.

Your role is to take care of them; their role is not to take care of your fear.

I treated an eight-year-old girl in play therapy for several years. Her father worked as a salesman and frequently traveled away from home. Her mother, not surprisingly, often felt lonely. Rather than address the issue with her husband, she turned to her daughter for emotional support. She refused to confront her husband, instead choosing to take the easy way out by encouraging her daughter to become her friend. During one session, I met with both mother and daughter. The mother began to complain about her husband's being away once again, and her daughter walked up to her, began stroking her mother's hair, and said, "Don't worry, Mommy. I'll take care of you." I knew from that one exchange that the mother needed therapy just as much as her daughter did, if not more so. You cannot be a good parent unless you choose to be an adult, which means facing your adult problems no matter how upsetting they may be to you.

If you are a grandparent and have developed a fear addiction, demanding that your children and grandchildren cater to your fears, it's time to take on the responsibility of the family elder role. You are old. You may die soon. Death comes for us all, and living in fear does not protect you from it. Do not begrudge your children and their children the gift of your company because you are afraid. Presumably, you have embraced adulthood before. You can do so again. Demanding that the young sacrifice their freedom, health, and opportunities to live a full life in order to "protect" the old is perverse and shameful. Do you want your legacy to be that of a coward, living his final years of life addicted to fear, demanding that his own family collude with immature, superstitious beliefs based on fantasies of immortality? You will be judged more on the application of what you learned at the end of your life than on how you behaved at the beginning of it. This is your opportunity to prove whether you have truly chosen to live as a mature adult or have simply grown old.

Equally important, if you have living parents yourself, do not pretend that you are acting responsibly by shunning them out of "concern for their safety." Rationalizing such cruel and insensitive behavior by embracing your addiction to fear is self-deception, and it is inexcusable. It is akin to committing murder in God's name, perhaps the gravest sin of all. Caring for your parents means fully including them in your life, regardless of how afraid you are. Establishing a proper way to care for them cannot include your fear. Living as an adult means not only living fully but also supporting others in their desire to live fully as well.

Everyone can come up with an endless supply of excuses, no matter their age, to avoid or postpone embracing adulthood. Fear has recently become the most common excuse because it is now the most socially acceptable. Despite what we have been told, however, fear is not virtuous, and fear is not a justification for remaining frozen in one's development. To properly care for others, you must set aside your fear, accept the discomfort that comes from assuming adult responsibilities, and choose to be an adult. Anything less is simply an act of collusion with your fear addiction. Fear addiction thrives on immaturity, irresponsibility, narcissism, and the denial of reality. Adulthood rejects all of this and clears the path for unlimited personal development, growth, and the attainment of one's individual potential.

Embrace adulthood. Establish a proper way to care for friends, family, and children.

Step 9

Overrule Your Emotions: Act in Spite of Your Fear

"I'm just not comfortable yet being with large groups of people." I heard this most recently from a teenage patient who had been kept from school for nearly two years due to closures and who is now allowed to return to school and extracurriculars such as sports, music, and theater. I was surprised that he wasn't overjoyed at the possibility of returning to the activities he had enjoyed two years earlier. When I pursued it further, he could not come up with one convincing reason why he should stay away from large groups of people. He just didn't feel ready. He had decided to act according to how he was feeling, no matter how disconnected his feelings were from actual reality.

For many Americans, certainly all Americans who are addicted to fear, this path of decision-making has become the norm. Even therapists, who are trained to see their emotions as information rather than a set of orders, have proven utterly incapable of separating their feelings from their actions.

One psychoanalyst in training who works in my building simply disappeared for over a year. When he returned, I didn't see his face for nearly another year. Whether I ran into him in the hall, the elevator, or the outdoor courtyard, all that was visible was a giant duck-bill mask. He told me, "I'm still struggling to go back to the office in person." Several other therapists in the building apparently are also "struggling" because they no longer leave their homes without their masks. As far as I can tell, they have no plans of ever removing them from their faces.

These people will never overcome their fear addiction as long as they maintain allegiance to their emotions, rather than simply accept that we all experience emotions all the time and that they need not determine our actions. Emotions are like waves of water coursing through us. They might move us briefly, depending on their strength, but they should never dictate our direction of movement. We should rely on our thoughts to chart our course. We should move in the direction we choose to, not in the direction we feel we should.

Making important decisions based solely on emotion is a universally bad practice. We have little control over our emotions, and they change often. Our emotions often reflect our recent decisions, good or bad. Perhaps you've decided to lose weight, and part of your weight-loss plan includes eating fewer desserts. While waiting in line for lunch one day, you may desire a dessert you see in the display case. After purchasing and eating it, though, you feel defeated and ashamed. You decided to eat the dessert based on how you were feeling in the moment rather than sticking with your plan. If you had waited thirty minutes before buying the dessert, would you still have wanted it?

Deferring gratification requires disregarding momentary feelings and honoring previously made decisions based on carefully constructed values and principles. Certainly, one impulsive food purchase will not ruin your life, but if the majority of your decisions come from how you feel in the moment, you will guarantee yourself a life of misery and suffering.

Overruling emotions when choosing your actions is fundamental to making good choices. Unchecked anger may lead to violence. Uncontrolled lust may lead to sexual infidelity. Fear, when it is given free rein and veto power over day-to-day life, inevitably produces avoidance and paralysis. Fear always should be acknowledged, but it should never be giving orders.

The emotion we know as fear, though, is quite powerful. It is more powerful than either love or hate. That is why it has the potential to exert such a strong influence over behavior. Traditionally, parents taught their children to not give in to fear. They did not deny its existence, but they made it clear that fear is never a reason to choose not to do something. In fact, parents rewarded their children for acting even when afraid—that is the definition of courage. Acting when you feel afraid, especially when you have something to lose, is the embodiment of courage. Without it, no one can achieve his potential.

No society can grow and thrive without its people displaying courage. I rarely see parents encouraging this virtue now. "If you don't feel comfortable, you don't have to do it," is the common refrain today. Elevating one's subjective emotional state over virtuous action has enabled fear addiction to spread.

The mother of a twelve-year-old patient of mine with autism fears her son's tantrums when he isn't given the food he wants. The boy is obese. At his last visit, she told me that when he threatened to act up the day before, she fed him five pizzas. "His anger scares me so much. I have no choice," she said. She does have a choice, though. Her choice is whether or not to stand up to her child and protect him from his own self-harm. But she allows her fear to decide for her, and the decisions she makes reinforce injury to her son.

The only way to succeed in denying fear the authority to dictate your actions is to develop a tolerance for uncomfortable feelings. That capacity is called *emotional resilience*. Poor emotional resilience in Americans has led to catastrophic social problems.

The pandemic of gender identity disorder—transgenderism—is driven largely by a culture that seeks to deny the reality of teenagers' feeling uncomfortable about who they are and the adults they are becoming. The process of solidifying an identity as a human being is a painful one. Despite what the transgender activists would have us believe, that discomfort cannot be avoided simply by a person's declaring himself to be a different gender. Identity is not declared. It is not defined by "identification." It is built, slowly and painfully, and often by taking risks while feeling afraid. There are no shortcuts.

I frequently hear the following from Americans of all ages: "I feel offended." "I feel unsafe." "I feel threatened." My reaction? Grow up. No one can "make" you feel anything. You cannot be offended without choosing to be. Feeling unsafe and feeling threatened are meaningless experiences in the absence of an objective threat. They are certainly irrelevant in determining how others should behave. Your responsibility is to develop emotional muscle to deal with these feelings without running away from life or wielding them as weapons against others. Treat your fear the same way. Do not suppress it, but do not allow it to guide what you say and do. It is purely information, and it may not even be accurate.

This may come as a shock to some but we are not meant to feel good all the time. In addition to providing information, feelings motivate us to act if we harness them correctly. The grief we experience in losing someone we love, for example, should encourage us to reflect on the loss. It directs our attention away from the outside world and toward the inside of ourselves so that we can truly feel the meaning of the loss. It is not pleasant or comfortable, but it is necessary.

Avoidance of grief may protect us from temporary emotional discomfort, but it blocks our ability to appreciate what we have lost. It arrests our development. On the other extreme, a protracted state of grief leads to depression, which is an emotional illness. While you are in a state of depression, you lose perspective. Just as a carnival house of mirrors distorts the way a body appears, depression magnifies negative perceptions and reduces or eliminates positive ones. Whereas grief brings life into sharp focus, depression turns everything gray and fuzzy. It is an anti–life force. Depression does not foster reflection, learning, or growth. It, too, leads to arrested development.

A corporate executive in her late forties came to me frustrated by her inability to advance further in her career. "As one of the leaders of the company, I'm often asked to make presentations to large groups at work," she told me, "but I am so afraid to stand up in front of people and speak that I feel paralyzed." She went on to describe how her face flushes, she feels dizzy, and she loses her ability to speak as soon as she takes the podium. "I'm not even capable of getting through a meeting with the board of directors without feeling an overwhelming need to run from the room and hide in the bathroom," she said.

I had to explain to her that feeling anxious when placing yourself at the center of attention of a crowd of people—especially people who can influence your career—is perfectly normal. The anxiety provoked by taking that risk is necessary to tap into your full capabilities. Being overly relaxed and lackadaisical would likely lead to errors and an unimpressive performance. I suggested that she not suppress the fear or try to run from it, but that she embrace it as proof that she is taking the assignment seriously. The sensations that erupt in her body as she stands up to face the room are not dangerous. They will not kill her. I encouraged her to let them flow through her and to continue to speak anyway. "Once you have experienced for yourself the fear of speaking and having survived it unscathed, the next time will be that much easier," I told her. I encouraged her to feel the fear and act in spite of it.

Few of us struggle with positive emotions. Joy, pleasure, triumph, love—we receive these emotions willingly. They feel good. They cost us nothing, in the short term, anyway. But they cannot exist in the absence of their opposites. How would we know, much less appreciate, joy if we do not know sadness? Addiction is a con because it focuses solely on behaviors that produce an immediate and short-term feeling of pleasure or thrill without the possibility of any unpleasant experience. That is, of course, impossible to achieve. Addiction peddles nirvana here on Earth. Fear addiction promises absolute safety—immortality—at the undisclosed cost of a full life.

We all know that couple who are joined at the hip. Everywhere one goes, the other goes as well. They complete each other's sentences. They never sleep apart. They often work together. Inseparable, they frequently declare how in love they are with each other. Yet something feels off. Are they really that in love? What we are probably sensing is the lack of individuation in each half of the couple. We see the couple, but we do not see the individuals. They have merged into one. They have confused togetherness with intimacy. But how can there be true intimacy between two people without some experience of separation and disconnection?

I would argue that fear of experiencing disconnection, rather than actual love, is what drives the commitment to their relationship. The individuals in this couple believe that by never leaving each other alone, they can forever protect themselves from loneliness. Imagine the catastrophe that would await them if one were to decide to end the relationship or pass away. In the meantime, only limited growth is possible because both people have insulated themselves from the conscious experience of negative emotions through the protective cocoon of the couple. Essentially, they are married to fear rather than to each other. Fear is the glue that binds them together, just as it is the chain that constrains their independent movement and growth as individuals.

How do we take the bad with the good? How do we tolerate the unknown without selling our souls to fear through the false bargain of exchanging freedom for security? We do it by building resilience—emotional muscle. Just as regular exercise is critical to building and maintaining physical strength, and as ongoing environmental exposure is critical to building and maintaining a healthy immune system, placing ourselves in emotionally "risky" situations is necessary to overcome fear.

The worst thing you can do when confronting an irrational fear is to walk right up to it, fail to confront it, and then walk away. If a young man fears rejection from women, approaching a woman he is interested in, saying nothing, and leaving simply reinforces the imaginary wall he is building that separates him from women. With every experience of cowardice, his will to challenge that fear grows weaker. What he must do is confront the invisible force field that imprisons him and then walk through it. He will survive. And then he will realize that the wall does not exist outside his own mind. The sense of accomplishment will embolden him to tackle other obstacles generated by his fear. Over time, if he continues in his quest, he will vanquish each of them.

A patient of mine in his early twenties had developed an addiction to nicotine vapes. At first, he found relief from the device and the nicotine it provided him. He would use it during his lunch break at work and then return feeling refreshed and ready to tackle the second half of the day. Slowly, though, his desire for nicotine increased until he found himself skulking away from his desk nearly every hour to furtively take one more hit—in the bathroom stall, in the emergency stairwell, in the elevator. He began to feel ashamed of the degree of control the drug had over him.

Although it wasn't true, it felt to him that he would not survive without regular nicotine infusions. Over several months, multiple times he considered and then abandoned the idea of confronting his addiction and discontinuing use entirely. After three or four failed attempts to act, it became nearly impossible for him to succeed. He had allowed his feelings to override what he knew was best for him. He would not feel his fear and act in spite of it.

If you are still rationalizing your failure to take the actions you know to be necessary to live a fearless life, telling yourself that you just don't feel ready, stop it immediately. You have become your worst enemy. How you feel is irrelevant. All that matters is what you do. Start small. Remove your mask the next time you enter a building. Note the anxiety that brings but also acknowledge when you exit that you're just fine. You have survived—unscathed. The next time you are introduced to someone, extend your hand.

Yes, it may be scary. But you will feel confident and more accomplished for having done it. Rather than placing your next order on Amazon drive to a store and buy the item in person. Say hello to the employees. Speak to the cashier when you check out. Once you've engaged with your human environment again, no matter how uncomfortable it made you feel, it will be that much easier the next time. It is easy to make excuses to hide from the world and bathe yourself in fear, but it is both gratifying and freeing to reengage. It will bring you a sense of connection, meaning, and purpose. You will never want to return to the life of fear that you were living before.

Overrule your emotions. Act in spite of your fear.

Step 10

Find Perspective: Develop a Sense of Humor

The barista at my local Coffee Bean never laughs anymore. I first noticed it when I overheard other customers say something funny and she didn't respond. "She must be having a bad day," I thought. The next time I came in, though, she displayed the same terse expression. I challenged myself to see if I could make her laugh. I brought out my best material. Not even a hint of a smile. She remained utterly unmoved.

I began to notice this phenomenon everywhere I went. Places I had previously found to be staffed by warm, friendly faces had metamorphosized into tense, anxious spaces. It was as if a transformation had occurred underneath all the masks after two years of incessantly wearing them. What had emerged was ugly, uncomfortable, and certainly no fun to be around.

Frozen faces. Blank stares. Dead eyes. There may be a physical reason for the disappearance of smiles for two years—universal masking. Now, though, the masks have largely come off, yet smiles are nearly as rare as they were at the height of the mask craze. The lack of their reappearance has a psychological cause rooted in the loss of perspective for those addicted to fear. Humor has become one more casualty of the pandemic.

Those addicted to fear have lost a sense of perspective. Their obsessional focus on "safety" has deprived them of the experience of life. A state of fear reorients one's focus toward survival, to the exclusion of all else. Just as a gambling addict is always thinking of how to score the next big win, the fear addict is eternally preoccupied with what steps to take to guarantee safety. This loss of perspective allows the fear to remain front and center, crowding out other aspects of life that provide real meaning. Also eliminated are opportunities to learn and grow, as everything in life is now seen through the lens of fear. This leads to a universal closing off of the self in a misguided attempt to protect, which is what I saw in the Coffee Bean barista and countless other retail service workers as businesses reopened in early 2022.

During my residency training in psychiatry, a cognitive behavioral therapy (CBT) supervisor explained to me what he called the "CBT triangle." He drew a triangle and wrote a word at each of the three points: "humor," "sex," and "anxiety." "Only one point of the triangle can be occupied at a given time," he said. "Someone in a state of anxiety does not feel amused or sexual. Someone who is laughing is not worried or expressing erotic energy. And someone who is sexually aroused is certainly not laughing or tense."

I've often thought about that triangle with my patients, as I find it a simple yet effective way to show how one emotional state can interfere with others. There is no one "best" emotional state to be in. We're meant to rotate through multiple states at different times. That is how we experience a full life. That is how we find perspective. Being locked into only one state for a long period of time deprives us of the opportunity to develop perspective.

Perspective is important because it allows us to step outside of ourselves and experience a reset that can lead to new thoughts. Much is made of "mindfulness" and being "in the moment." There is certainly something to be gained by minimizing distractions and directing focus on the now. What if the now, though, is nothing more than a perpetual fearful rumination? A soil of fear does not produce life—it paralyzes it. When this happens, one of the most powerful methods available to break free from the grip of fear is a change in perspective. And the fastest way to achieve that is through humor.

Humor is like perspective shock therapy. It always comes as a surprise. Jokes that are funny surprise us. The best comedians deliver punch lines that no one saw coming. They surprise the members of their audience—who are there to be surprised—with a sudden revealing of a different way of looking at things, leaving everyone energized and excited, utterly unconcerned about the problems facing them as individuals and the world at large.

The audience at a comedy club may arrive anxious but leaves enlivened. Social distance disappears. Social connection grows. Good comedy frees people from their stuck, fixed perspectives and reveals new ways of approaching and participating in life. It is nearly impossible to leave a great comedy routine feeling afraid.

The fearful always lack perspective. The best examples of this are those who suffer from post-traumatic stress disorder (PTSD). Clint Eastwood played an aging former soldier with untreated PTSD in the film *Gran Torino*.

During the day, he numbed his fear by drinking, sitting on the front porch of his house with a cooler of beer, methodically making his way through one after another, until the sun went down. At night he slept next to his loaded rifle, and when he heard a noise outside, he would instantly jump out of bed, grab the gun, and begin his perimeter patrol. Psychologically, he returned to wartime, when his mission was to seek out and confront the enemy. The stakes could not be higher: life or death.

He lived this way for years, consumed by fear, unable to grow and develop. His fear precluded him from developing any new perspective since returning from war. He also was utterly humorless. Nothing made him smile or laugh. He had found himself occupying the fear-and-anxiety point on the CBT triangle and could not surrender it.

It's important not to confuse sarcasm and mockery with humor. Humor opens the door to new perspectives. Sarcasm and mockery close it. The reason why nearly all late-night television comedy shows are no longer funny is that their hosts know only how to mock and ridicule. You can listen to hours of their talking and leave with nothing other than your existing views having been reinforced, or if you disagree with what they are saying, an overwhelming sense of disgust.

Johnny Carson may have been the last consistently funny late-night comedy show host because he always surprised his audience with his jokes. You never knew where he stood politically. He would poke fun at public figures, but he never mocked them. He challenged conventional thinking rather than reinforced it. He did not come across as angry or bitter, like David Letterman, Stephen Colbert, and Trevor Noah do. His mission was to make people laugh, and he truly understood humor.

I know from my own clinical experience that the most fearful patients are also the most humorless. They cannot see anything through a lens not tainted by fear. Perspective is absent. Often, they are unreachable. At the extreme, fear transforms into paranoia. A person with paranoia views all competing perspectives as threats.

One young adult patient suffered from paranoid delusions for several years before seeing me. She believed she was the victim of witchcraft. Her parents were furious that she had spent thousands of dollars on astrology readings as a form of treatment for her illness. Fortunately, with the right treatment, she began to improve. I knew she had made real progress when I first heard her tell a joke in my office. Soon, she began to find it funny that she had ever believed in witches or that she had relied on an astrologer to guide her life.

Maintaining a different perspective and protecting it through humor has become one of her greatest strengths. Despite her predisposition to paranoid delusions, she fared far better during the lockdowns than her mother, a neurotic woman who struggled to find anything at all to laugh at.

Humor and laughter are antidotes to fear and anxiety. Is it any surprise that live jokes were effectively outlawed for nearly two years in most parts of the United States? Comedy clubs were closed in 2020 and have only recently begun to reopen. Many have been permanently shuttered. Of course, severing human connections encourages fear to take root and spread, but eliminating laughter has had just as odious an effect on society. Smiles are invisible behind a mask. Humor and laughter deprive fear of its potency. The worst possible reaction of an audience watching a horror movie in a theater is laughing at the monster. And just as fear is infectious, so is laughter. Once the perspective that there is nothing to fear begins to spread, it becomes difficult to return to a state of fear.

Whereas fear and humor are like oil and water—they cannot mix—tragedy and humor frequently find themselves companions, one sharpening the other. Humor can be the tool that prevents tragedy from evolving into depression. Is it an accident that the greatest American comedians of the twentieth century were Jews? Or that the most famous satirists often come from the most repressive states, like the Soviet Union? Jews and dissidents—and dissident Jews—have harnessed the power of humor to build and disseminate a perspective that assigns meaning to tragedy.

Essentially, humor breaks down programming, a consequence of fear addiction. Every patient with fear addiction I see operates on a single track. These people have no time or space to devote to anything that does not support or reinforce their irrational preoccupation with "staying safe." Their thinking is robotic and reflexive.

I attended a fiftieth birthday party for a friend. It was held in her home, with nearly one hundred people in attendance. Several caterers served different foods, and she hired a bartender to prepare drinks. Not one person, including the staff, wore a mask, except for two girls making crepes at the dessert station. When I went to get my crepe, I asked them if their employer required this. They said no. "So why, then, are you wearing masks on your faces? You know the couple who are paying you would prefer that you don't, and none of the guests are wearing masks. None of the other workers are wearing masks. You're both young and appear healthy. Why?" One of them stared at me blankly for several seconds before replying, "We think it's more respectful."

Not once the entire night did I see either of them smile, laugh, or engage with anyone at the party. They did their job, served their crepes, and then cleaned up and left. Like compliant, unquestioning robots, they were not open to a new perspective. They were not open to simply taking in the moment, surrounded by friendly, fearless people. Their programming would not allow them to experience joy, humor, or laughter.

Finding perspective and developing a sense of humor do not need to be difficult. It starts with simply orienting to your immediate surroundings and training your awareness to focus on what is actually happening now—to you, to others near you, to your environment. It starts with paying attention. This is different from perseverating on your own internal dialogue and projecting it outward onto anyone and anything you see. It demands a certain receptivity and openness to take in whatever information your senses are collecting. You must relinquish control over your environment and accept that you have very little influence over what will happen.

Once you do this, you'll start to notice details that were invisible before. Idiosyncrasies and incongruencies will capture your attention. You may notice the dog walking by with a tortilla in his mouth at the party or the woman ordering a Diet Coke with her chocolate cake at the café. When you observe unique details, your perspective will shift. You may find yourself laughing at things you had never noticed before. And as you're laughing, you will temporarily forget to feel afraid.

Go to a comedy club. Go even if you're afraid to. Challenge yourself. If you can allow yourself to laugh, you will temporarily interrupt the fear programming and provide yourself with the opportunity to explore a new perspective. This may be so freeing that you'll feel encouraged to return.

Play a game—if you have children, you have a ready-made team. If not, invite your adult friends over for a game night. Find something freeing and creative that uses language or drawing rather than knowledge-testing or cutthroat strategy. The best games allow you to get to know more about the people you're playing with and allow them to get to know more about you. Being surprised by the discoveries you are all making will necessarily bring in new perspectives and probably a lot of laughter as well.

Watch old cartoons. Warner Brothers and Disney have made some of the funniest cartoons ever. If you watched them only as a child, watch them again. They contain multiple layers, and some of those layers are revealed only to adult eyes. They will make you laugh and tell yourself, "I never saw that before." One of the main lessons cartoons teach children is to laugh and not be afraid, even when things look ominous. Adults could use that lesson, too.

The fastest and most powerful way to find a new perspective is through humor. It is accessible to anyone, young or old, educated or not. It is the great social equalizer. It reminds us of our fallibility, our foibles, and our relative insignificance in the greater scheme of things. It does so not with violence or cruelty but through a gentle nudge of a new perspective. It invites us to set aside our programming, our rigidity, and our loyalty to how we think we are supposed to feel or think. It provides us with a respite from the heaviness of life and, perhaps, freedom from our fear.

Find perspective. Develop a sense of humor.

Step 11

Pay Attention: Give the Gift of Your Full Presence

For well over a year, I had seen two of my child patients, who were brothers, only through Zoom. Their parents had become addicted to fear and would not bring either one to my office. I had been speaking mainly with the father, who had assured me everything was going well at home. One day the mother brought the two boys to my office. She admitted to having developed a fear addiction but also explained that she had worked very hard to overcome it. Now she was ready to return to an emotionally healthy life, and she wanted to help her children do that as well.

What concerned her most, though, was the disconnection she felt from her husband. "He won't participate in the family game night that I organize," she told me. "All he wants to do is watch TV by himself. It's like he's not really there." Her husband, although he had continued to work, had withdrawn his attention from the family. He had used fear as a rationalization for disconnecting. His wife felt frustrated, hurt, and demoralized.

I cannot overstate the importance of giving your full presence to others—whether to strangers, family members, or friends. In late 2021 I visited a man who had relocated from California to Texas, in part to offer his wife and two young children a healthier environment. His wife homeschools both children. I was shocked and impressed by the level of social interaction between the children and the adults in the home, including with other guests staying there. The children were polite and friendly. They also expressed their needs without hesitation, made eye contact, and asked the adult guests questions, showing they were clearly paying attention. They also were clearly unafraid.

When I asked the father to explain how his children had developed so well, he said, "I've really made a strong effort personally to be a good model for them." He told me how he had caught himself once brushing off his son when the boy had come to him with a question about homework: "I didn't even look at him when I told him I was busy. Fortunately, I caught myself right away, turned to him, and said, 'I'm busy working on something right now. In about a half-hour, I'll be done, and I'll let you know so we can work on this together.' I'm convinced that giving him my full attention for thirty seconds is far more valuable to him than sitting next to him for thirty minutes distracted by the messages coming through my phone." This father, a fearless man, has taught his boys the importance of being fully present with others.

Going through life in a state of semidisconnection from people certainly is not new. Smartphones, ADHD, lack of work boundaries, and videoconferencing all have led to an erosion in attention. Paying attention is a skill that tends to deteriorate when not used.

Even before 2020, I had seen a steady decline in my patients' ability to be present in the room with me. One adult patient who worked for a well-known Los Angeles talent agency, for example, arrived ten minutes late to every appointment, was always on his phone when I greeted him in the waiting room, and often interrupted our conversation to glance at his phone during the session. His primary concern was feeling constantly overwhelmed, exhausted, and unable to be with his family in the evenings without his mind wandering back to work. Most of my young adult patients set their oversized phones next to them on the couch when they sit down. Even after they silence their devices, the frequent vibrations clearly impair their focus on our conversations. Nearly everyone in my practice has been battling this problem of inattention for some time.

Recently, though, the problem has become far worse. Since 2020, a combination of fear and a revolution in legally enforced social norms has made it nearly impossible, in many circumstances, for people to consistently provide their full attention to others. This has been one of the greatest casualties of the government's response to the pandemic. The lack of simple acknowledgment of the existence of other human beings around us has nearly destroyed the American social fabric. In many urban areas, such as Los Angeles, where I live and work, you can spend a full day walking the streets and not encounter a single person who even looks at you. If you speak to someone, you will likely receive a mumbled, nearly unintelligible response. This sort of public behavior has become normative, expected, and acceptable.

At most restaurants here now, there are no menus. You order your food from the table using your phone and a QR code. No need to even speak with the waiter. Paying with cash is discouraged. "Contactless" payment is now the preferred—and often only—option. Many dine-in restaurants are now doing more business with takeout and delivery than they are with in-person dining. They have established a permanent curbside kiosk, where you use a computer to order and pay for your food and then wait outside for someone to hand you a bag, presumably so that you can then return home with it and eat by yourself in your apartment. Both restaurants and bars now offer "take-home cocktails" so that you can spare yourself the anxiety of engaging in actual conversation with others at the bar. The City of Los Angeles even has passed a law to allow for this to continue indefinitely. If you're eating alone, why not drink alone, too?

No matter where you live, if you have flown on a commercial airplane, you know how socially disconnected the experience has become. All airlines have reduced or eliminated food and beverage service on flights, even on coast-to-coast flights that last five hours or more. This is true regardless of how much you pay for your ticket.

Recently I flew first class on American Airlines from Los Angeles to Denver. All I received was coffee and my choice of crackers. In one of the more bizarre—and anti-social—air travel practices to begin since 2020, Southwest Airlines now requests that its passengers not speak to the flight crew during beverage service. Passengers are instructed to "just raise one finger for water, two for coffee, and three for soda." Of course, no passengers ever speak to one another now after taking their seats. That would be considered gauche.

Antisocial behaviors and practices had been mandated for so long that even with the removal of the mandates, the behaviors continue. Many people now feel anxious when standing near others. They avoid eye contact. They speak to strangers only when necessary. So many Americans have been wearing masks indoors and out that they have forgotten how to use their faces around others. The simple act of smiling has largely disappeared from day-to-day life here in Los Angeles. The withdrawal of attention in every social sphere has had a corrosive effect on American society. It has worsened the preexisting anxiety and depression of my patients. It has led to marital discord and, in single people, loneliness and feelings of rejection. These are the consequences to the individual and the group of living a life of fear for over two years. We have allowed our social norms to be set by the most fearful among us rather than the most courageous. By deferring to their fear, we are empowering it as an instrument of social control.

One of the hardest-hit populations is young adults. They were suffering from socialization challenges pre-2020, so their vulnerability to the effects of the fear pandemic was pronounced. For several years now, I have been offering advice to my young male patients who find themselves uncomfortable around women. When they go on dates, they often obsess over their fear that they won't know what to say. I explain to them that they misunderstand the goal of the date. They are not there to entertain, interrogate, or impress (through their talk, humor, or display of money or social status). Their purpose should be to make themselves 100 percent available to the woman for the duration of their encounter, in part by listening carefully and making sustained eye contact.

When they make establishing a connection their goal, the fear they experience shifts to a more peripheral location in their mind. Fear keeps the experience more about the young man and less about his date. When he shifts his attention to the woman while maintaining full receptivity to what she is offering him, he encourages a powerful connection that infuses the interaction with meaning. Mutual exploration hinges on the man's availability to take in the person he is with. That avenue is blocked when fear predominates.

Fear addicts believe they're paying attention, but they're not. Attending to someone through your presence and living in a state of fear are two mutually exclusive positions. The former invites the other person in. The latter shuts him out. All fear-driven behaviors interrupt attention and block access to being fully present. "Staying safe" has become the fear-driven rationalization for withdrawing oneself from full participation in the healthy social exchange of human beings. Few dare to challenge this pathology. Obeisance to fear is the new social norm.

Similar to a politician's plea for support of a corrupt initiative on the grounds that "it's for the children," the fear addict's defense of both personally and socially destructive behavior has become "safety." And who would ever challenge the necessity of respecting safety? An individual's emotional comfort has now become synonymous with safety. In fact, there is really no longer any distinction made between emotional safety and actual safety. An individual's inability to tolerate discomfort in standing near someone and making eye contact is not an expression of respect. It is a symptom of mental illness.

A woman I know lost her husband when he committed suicide. In the months following his death, those who knew her would approach her in the local grocery store and offer platitudes or empty words of sympathy, such as: "He's in a better place." "I understand how you feel." "Such a tragedy." Others would avoid her entirely, afraid to be in the presence of a grieving woman. Either way, she felt very alone, and not only from the loss of her husband. She became acutely aware of the unavailability of many of her friends and neighbors. They assumed either that they had nothing to offer her or that she expected them to provide her with a solution to her problem.

Neither was correct. All the woman wanted or expected from them was a moment of their presence and their attention. What she needed from them was their receptivity to her experience of shock, loss, and grief. Had she simply been asked sincerely, "How are you doing?" and then been listened to without interruption or comment, she would have left the encounter with a small amount of solace. If they had provided her their full attention, even for a moment, without offering a solution or a platitude, she would have felt seen and received, which is all that someone who is grieving really expects. Making sense of the death and coming to terms with it are her responsibility—no one else's. Suicide is a violent attack on relationships. For the one who is left behind, being reminded that other relationships continue is one of the most helpful experiences available. When anxiety or fear prevents that experience, the one who is grieving is deprived of necessary human connection when it is most needed.

Everyone—mourners, children, lovers and spouses, friends, family members—needs the attention of other human beings. This includes strangers in elevators, customers in stores, and patients in hospitals. When this attention is withdrawn, one of the most important threads in the fabric of social reciprocity is cut. Economies are built around the free exchange of goods and services. There is a social economy as well, and it is based on relationships. Those relationships are not built primarily by gifts and favors but by time spent together—quality time.

By quality time, I mean time spent in the full presence of each other. The only way to receive another person is by offering your full presence. If you are afraid, you will be closed off and unable to achieve that. You then not only will deprive others of real connection with you but also will handicap yourself. Fear reinforces isolation, leading to depression, resentment, and loss of perspective. It is antihuman. The opposite is receptivity, presence, and attention.

For many years, I practiced Brazilian jiujitsu. One of the first lessons I learned, and one that remained important no matter how far I progressed, was to reduce both physical and emotional tension when working with a partner. At first, my fear got in the way. I was worried about being hurt or hurting someone else. Slowly my confidence grew. My fear diminished. Eventually, I found it much easier to focus my awareness on my partner, take in his movements no matter how subtle, and then respond to them appropriately.

It took me a long time to deeply incorporate this into my training, but as I improved, I became a better training partner—safer and more helpful. Through a physical practice, I improved my emotional awareness. It became obvious after several years of training that fear and rigidity actually made it more difficult to stay safe, not less. This discovery is universal among all those who practice martial arts long enough, just as it is for surgeons who operate long enough. In my case, greater awareness led to fewer injuries, for myself and my partner. But I had to overcome my fear first.

Consistently offering your full presence is a practice that requires conscious effort and time. It demands repetition. It is a practice that directly challenges fear. The physical steps required—removing masks, eliminating physical distance—are only preparatory actions. Once those barriers are removed, you must generate a mindset that sets aside anxiety and fear—acknowledging these emotions but not giving them power—and make it your conscious priority to exercise your curiosity, your self-awareness, and your attention entirely on the person before you for the time you are together. This is an alive, responsive process that honors the connection between you and everyone around you, as well as your environment.

Fear thrives on separation. It feeds on not knowing and fills the vacuum generated by disconnection. By offering your presence, you banish fear by bridging the gap between you and the other person. You also provide an invaluable gift, which is the experience of being truly received.

This is not without risk. As your experiential knowledge of the other person grows, you may find that you dislike that person. You may even reject him at some point. What you will feel less of, though, is fear. Fear will be disarmed and disempowered through the repeated practice of maintaining awareness and attention. Paying attention—not turning away—is a powerful antidote to fear and fear addiction.

Pay attention. Give the greatest gift you can to another—your full presence.

Step 12

Display Fearless Leadership: Grow Your Courage by Mentoring Others

An elder woman came with her husband to see me. She already had made good progress in overcoming her fear, but she felt stuck. I asked her whether she had been participating in any community organizations. She had no answer. I explained to her that working all alone to overcome fear can be a difficult and lonely process. Not only did she need more support, but she needed an opportunity to use what she had learned by sharing it with others.

I happened to know of a group near her home with a reputation for fostering leadership and resisting fear. I suggested she join it. Shortly after, she became a member. Not long after that, she took on a leadership role in the organization. She flourished and abandoned what was left of her fear.

Not a single patient in my practice who had assumed a leadership role before 2020 has succumbed to fear addiction. It appears that acting as a leader serves as a potent inoculation against being infected by irrational fear. Leadership and fear addiction are mutually incompatible. The reason for this is complex and involves many factors. Essentially, though, leaders don't develop fear addiction because they are always practicing the steps described in this book.

Leadership incorporates all the steps necessary to combat fear addiction. It challenges narcissism, aids awareness and attention, generates accountability, and builds perspective. As with parenting, assuming the responsibility of guiding and inspiring others activates inner qualities that serve as potent anti-fear agents. Of course, not all parents act responsibly, just as not all leaders act honorably. Virtuous leadership, though, nearly always competes with fear.

In Alcoholics Anonymous, becoming a sponsor is an act of leadership and mentorship. Shepherding another through the steps of overcoming addiction reinforces one's own abstinence. In addition to giving back to the community, sponsorship strengthens and benefits the sponsor. It makes it difficult to hide in the group, and knowing that others are watching you creates motivation to honor the values you claim to hold. The antithesis is anonymity, by which you simply blend in with your environment. This encourages bad behavior, as anonymity removes all accountability. When you practice it with virtue, leadership isn't about you. It requires self-sacrifice, which builds loyalty. Supporting others brings support to you.

Displaying fearless leadership is the final step in overcoming fear addiction. This step cannot be completed until you have worked diligently on all the others. There are no shortcuts. A mentor who continues to suffer from unchecked narcissism will be unable to keep the needs of his mentee in mind. A leader who is unable to find humor in the mini tragedies of day-to-day life cannot provide the necessary perspective to inspire others to continue when faced with failure. The preparatory path must be followed first. One step at a time.

A retired woman, divorced and living alone, had spent several years healing from an abusive relationship with a man after her marriage dissolved. She also healed her body after developing cancer. Surrounding herself with like-minded and fearless people brought her essential support. Rather than listening to an unending barrage of fear porn masquerading as news, she began reading uplifting novels and well-researched articles on what is actually happening in the world. All that was missing was a place for her to engage with others who might not be as far along on the path as she was. She began volunteering at a local Jewish community center that offered financial, logistical, and psychological support services to drug addicts and the mentally ill. Her past professional experience in management became useful when she proposed new ways of organizing group support at the facility. She became a trainer at the center and found a new sense of purpose in life. Fully invigorated, she began to challenge the culture of fear that was holding back the recipients of services offered there. Today, it is hard to imagine her being susceptible to fear of any kind. She exemplifies fearless leadership through her ongoing mentorship at the community center.

There are many ways to be a leader. Most leaders are not born—they are made. Perhaps the most direct way to become a leader is to join a group where leaders are needed. Most groups suffer from a lack of leadership, so this should not be difficult. Simply volunteering to take on a leadership role will force you to use the capacities you have built by having worked the previous steps, as well as develop new ones. Churches and synagogues are excellent places to start. So are tennis clubs, if you prefer something athletic.

For those attracted to neither religion nor sports, book clubs provide a space for strangers to meet regularly to discuss ideas. If no groups where you live interest you, know that throughout the United States today, many people lack a vital, active group or club to belong to, so you are not alone. Start your own. You can begin by simply inviting people you know to your home for coffee and a place to talk or get a group together from work for a lunchtime walk or an after-work hike. The options are endless.

To be a leader, all it takes is a simple plan and a clear invitation to two or more people. You will build your courage, your competence, and your resilience. And you will put yourself in a position to be seen, which will automatically grow your social circle. It also may lead to new professional opportunities.

Some people prefer to lead indirectly. If you are skilled at writing, you can begin a weekly column and publish it—for free—on Substack. Your local paper also may need content. Is there a subject that you're passionate about and that others would appreciate reading about? Write a few sample columns and send them to the editor. You could become the community authority on gardening, pet care, or healthy eating. Using knowledge in a thoughtful way through writing can be a powerful method of establishing your leadership and influencing people both near and far.

Good writers also are in high demand as speakers. If you establish yourself, you may be invited to other cities and states, where you can meet people you otherwise wouldn't. Even if you have no ambition to spread your knowledge beyond your local town, you can still establish yourself where you live, with the option of opening your home to those who follow you, or set up a special-interest club based on your writing topic. You can pursue this in many different ways, depending on what your goals and passions are.

Teaching is an excellent way to lead and mentor. Companies of any size can benefit from in-house instruction. If you work at one, study a specific sector in your professional field, and you can become an expert. Then you can offer your expertise through training during the lunch hour. As long as you offer something of value, people will come, and then you will be seen as a resource in that field.

If you work in an occupation that has a professional organization attached to it, it is virtually guaranteed that you can find opportunities to teach—through conferences or symposia—simply by approaching the head of the local chapter. Although professional organizations may have many members, they often lack volunteer leadership. You will be welcomed with open arms. This method works equally well in most community organizations, such as churches and charities. It doesn't take much to know more about a specific area than nearly everyone else. The knowledge you have to share will open up more opportunities for leadership than simply attending conferences as a member of the audience.

I have been mentoring others for many years. Before beginning medical school, I founded a tutoring company in the San Francisco Bay Area. I went to the homes of high school students and helped them with English, French, math, and physics. I discovered that their needs were less academic than they were interpersonal. Much of my time was spent listening to their problems in getting along with parents, friends, and teachers.

One girl in San Francisco, whom I visited to work on her English essays, admitted that she had grown fond of drinking Jack Daniel's in the evening so she wouldn't have to engage with her mother, whom she always fought with. Another was frequently brought to tears by her math assignments. She explained to me that her parents were Russian immigrants and expected her to score 100 percent on every test. "That's how they were raised, but they don't understand how different it is here," she told me. I helped both young women find better ways to communicate with their parents. Their grades magically improved. More than tutoring, what they really needed was sound advice from an adult outside the family. They began to thrive once they received it.

Later in medical school and throughout my residency, I taught medical students and other residents. Many were frightened at the prospect of working with psychiatric patients. They wondered, "Will they attack me?" "What if they try to kill themselves?" I worked hard to dispel the common myths that stigmatize the field of psychiatry, explaining that the mentally ill were suffering just as much as the physically ill and that they needed even more empathy because they often felt isolated and alone. Finding ways to allay the fears of the trainees strengthened my own conviction that fear may affect us all, but we need not allow it to take over.

I continued teaching after opening my clinical practice, giving lectures to therapists in training at a local program in Los Angeles. I also supervised pre-licensed therapists by discussing their cases with them. They often were anxious, felt a lack of confidence, and worried that they weren't doing what was necessary to help their patients. One young therapist had trouble sleeping at night because a child she was seeing often cut herself and threatened suicide. I reminded her that regardless of the outcome, were the child to receive no help, the situation would have been even worse. These trainees came to me to find perspective. To be able to offer that to them strengthened my confidence and reminded me of how far I had come from my own early days of training, when I was the one feeling anxious and scared. It felt gratifying to know that I could make a difference in the lives of future licensed therapists simply by guiding them through the emotional minefield of working with difficult patients.

Perhaps dealing with fearful and anxious people for so many years has inoculated me to most fear, and certainly to all irrational fear. In my office, I sit across from patients every day and listen to their stories, often filled with emotional catastrophes, and I try to simultaneously empathize with them and not be pulled into the whirlpool of emotion that has overwhelmed them. The natural tendency of an empathic listener is to resonate emotionally with the person he is listening to. When the resonance is at the level of fear, both parties get swept away and lose their ability to think clearly.

Just as a good therapist avoids this trap, a good mentor or leader will make every effort to quell the fear in the room and replace it with calm, thoughtful reflection. He will not make any recommendations for action in the name of fear but in the name of freedom from fear. That should be the goal of every leader, every teacher, and every mentor: to free others from fear and encourage healthy action. By practicing leadership, the leader sharpens his own skill in avoiding being taken by fear. He leads by example, showing that fear is not guiding his decisions or his actions. He conquers his own fear addiction by helping others overcome theirs.

Display fearless leadership. Grow your courage by mentoring others.

Conclusion

Towards a National Recovery

I am often asked, "How do we repair our nation?" I am convinced that the answer does not lie in a top-down but rather a bottom-up approach. This is why individual recovery is crucial if we are to have any hope of national reform.

Our institutions are corrupt: the federal government, national corporations, and legacy media. They have conspired together for over two years to further their own interests at the expense of the American people. They have lied, stolen, and murdered. They—not a Chinese virus—have been responsible for nearly all of the pandemic deaths. By instilling fear, bankrupting businesses, denying medical care, and force-injecting poison into the arms of tens of millions of Americans, all in the name of "health and safety," they have brought the United States nearly to its knees. Our nation is now on the verge of collapse.

And there is no savior coming, no knight on a white horse. If we continue to wait for one, we will lose. This country was founded on the distrust of government and centralized power and on a reverence for the citizenry's full participation in the context of institutional checks and balances. Our government was designed to be one of the people and for the people, not an autocracy or an oligarchy. We have never had a king, an emperor, or a politburo in charge of our lives. Now we do.

Our salvation will not come from the top but rather from the bottom. Civic and political institutions need to first be reformed at the local level. Noncareer politicians must run for city councils. Mothers with children in the schools must run for city school boards. The successful return of power to the people in Virginia's Loudoun County and San Francisco by the unseating of activist ideologues from the local school boards must spread throughout the United States. And then the winners of these elections must grow and learn, move up the ladder, and take back the county and state offices, cleaning house as they go. Eventually, they will arrive in Washington, D.C., for a massive federal cleanup in preparation for the dismantling of the deep state that exerts an enormous concentrated power with no accountability. It must be removed if the nation is to return to health.

How can this book help?

To recover as a nation, we must first recover as individuals. Alcoholics Anonymous is not a federal agency or program. It is a collection of local, self-supported groups in communities across the country, all working independently but guided by the same set of beliefs and principles. AA is ubiquitous, highly effective, and entirely voluntary. It has done more to aid Americans in recovering from alcohol addiction than any government venture.

Fear addiction also must be treated locally, one American at a time. The steps described here can guide Americans in overcoming their fear addiction, so they can return to their family and to their professional and civic lives with renewed purpose and a focus on what really matters. A population that has overcome its addiction to fear can then reinstitute healthy social norms, begin to rebuild local institutions, and engage politically with clarity and wisdom. Just as the Great Awakening brought participation in religion back to the American colonies in the early 1700s, the United States today is in desperate need of a populist revival that will restore the key concepts of freedom and liberty to our local communities, one by one. That can be accomplished only by a population that is no longer living in fear.

The fear pandemic was mandated by the state. The recovery from fear must be initiated by the citizenry. *Freedom From Fear* is the individual's guide to leading our nation to recovery, one American at a time.

About the Author

Photo Credit: *Mikki Willis*

Born and raised in Los Angeles, Mark McDonald graduated from UC Berkeley before attending medical school at the Medical College of Wisconsin. Trained in both adult and child and adolescent psychiatry at UCLA, he now works primarily with children in private practice in west Los Angeles. Dr. McDonald has lived and worked in Europe, Asia, and Central America. His opinions on topics such as the need to re-open America's schools, and the pandemic of fear in the United States today, have been widely published in local and national news, including the *Wall Street Journal* and *The Federalist*.